FISHING TACKLE • PERRY D. FRAZER

Publisher's Note

The book descriptions we ask booksellers to display prominently warn that this is an historic book with numerous typos or missing text; it is not indexed or illustrated.

The book was created using optical character recognition software. The software is 99 percent accurate if the book is in good condition. However, we do understand that even one percent can be an annoying number of typos! And sometimes all or part of a page may be missing from our copy of the book. Or the paper may be so discolored from age that it is difficult to read. We apologize and gratefully acknowledge Google's assistance.

After we re-typeset and design a book, the page numbers change so the old index and table of contents no longer work. Therefore, we often remove them; otherwise, please ignore them.

We carefully proof read any book that will sell enough copies to pay the proof reader; unfortunately, most don't. So instead we try to let customers download a free copy of the original typo-free book. Simply enter the barcode number from the back cover of the paperback in the Free Book form at www.RareBooksClub.com. You may also qualify for a free trial membership in our book club to download up to four books for free. Simply enter the barcode number from the back cover onto the membership form on our home page. The book club entitles you to select from more than a million books at no additional charge. Simply enter the title or subject onto the search form to find the books.

If you have any questions, could you please be so kind as to consult our Frequently Asked Questions page at www. RareBooksClub.com/faqs.cfm? You are also welcome to contact us there.

General Books LLC™, Memphis, USA, 2012. ISBN: 9780217211710.

-:- -:- -:- -:- -:- -:- -:- -:-

FISHING TACKLE CHAPTER I WORK AND RECREATION IN THE CLOSED SEASON

A one of the fly-and-bait-casting tournaments of the National Association of Scientific Angling Clubs, a visitor who had been an angler all his life, but who desired to become proficient in casting with the fly-rod, asked if, in purchasing a tournament fly-rod, it would be advisable for him to begin with a rod of say nine feet and eight ounces, practice with it awhile, then purchase one of ten or eleven feet, and so on, his idea being that he would be sure to get the wrong sort of a rod at first, but would ultimately learn what was best. There are thousands of anglers who view the purchase of fishing tackle in this light I am well aware. To them it seems that there is something mysterious connected with rods and tackle and that they can only master details after wasting some money.

To a great many anglers, too, the idea of repairing their own rods and tackle seems impossible, while as for making little odds and ends of constant usefulness, this is believed to be a task to be looked at only in the light of certain failure.

In my little workshop I have a few simple tools with which I have made a number of articles, which if not handsome, have at least given me the greatest satisfaction when they proved to be practical. There are very few anglers who cannot do even better work. During the long evenings of autumn and winter a great deal of amusement may be obtained from overhauling the fishing rods and tackle, making little devices for use the next season, and giving the weary brain change and rest from the exactions of one's daily toil.

Just to show how the angler may experiment along the lines that fascinate him, I will mention a new reel which, while from one of the best makers, did not act just as I thought it should. All of the parts were beautifully made and fitted, but there was tremendous vibration during a cast, and in my own way I reasoned that the handle was at fault. Not wishing to mar this, I removed it, and searching through a box of junk, found a scrap of aluminum about half as thick as the German silver handle of the reel. Laying the handle on this scrap, I traced its outline with a scratch-awl, but made it shorter than the factory handle, then, with a tiny saw cut just outside the lines, filed the edges smooth, bored a hole in the center and squared this to fit the handle-post.

Holes were drilled, in one end for a finger knob and in the other for a counter-weight. The knob was made from a piece of brass rod. The head of a round-head screw was cut off and filed until it would just balance the knob when the new handle was laid across one edge of a three-square file. Both the screw-head and the knob were riveted in place, the handle made fast on the post, and timing the reel with my watch, I found that it would spin twenty-six seconds without appreciable vibration, whereas with the original handle it would spin only seventeen seconds, and the vibration was disagreeable in casting.

This work took more than an hour, but while the reel was improved for my use, no harm had been done the original handle. The manufacturer probably had a certain number of handles made, and used this one, which answered the purpose in a general way, but was not of the best weight or length for that particular reel. A little careful investigation was worth while in this instance. Any angler possessing ordinary skill can make a better handle than mine—and this is true of nearly all repairs and improvements in rods and tackle. Besides, there is a satisfaction in overcoming a difficulty yourself instead of leaving it to someone else.

CHAPTER II OVERHAULING THE TACKLE-BOX WITH the passing of the winter anglers begin to make plans for the next fishing season. And although the nights gradually grow shorter, it is not until half of the winter has passed, and the nights are cold, and it is so pleasant to stay indoors and tinker until bedtime, that one feels like settling down to doing something with his fishing outfit. If the veteran anglers find in the chapters that follow any matter that is ancient history to them, they will, I know, be charitable enough to admit that beginners search diligently through books and papers for information of this sort, and they deserve all the consideration and encouragement that we can give them. Even some of the veterans, it is

hoped, may find here a wrinkle or two worth remembering; for in all walks of life we find persons who say they are "not handy" at doing this or that thing, and thereby lose a lot of pleasure. For it is real pleasure, and a source of lasting satisfaction as well, to any angler to repair his own tackle, and all through the active season he can make mental notes of the changes which his experience tells him he should make " next winter."

The alterations made are those decided on after long consideration, and half the pleasure of accomplishment would be lost were someone else allowed to do the tinkering planned for winter pastime. The rodmaker can hardly do these small jobs, for if minor changes must be made by a professional, the chances are that they will not be made at all, new articles being purchased instead. One cannot as well explain how he wants a thing done as to tinker it out himself. And the tackle dealer who keeps repair materials and fittings reaps his profit on these articles in the dull season.

The first thing to do is to lay out the entire fishing kit and make a detailed survey and inventory. If a new rod is decided on, write down its specifications, while your ideas are fresh, at the end of the season's fishing. Go over the old rods and recall their faults, so that the new one may be different. Then give the order for the new one to your rodmaker, so that he may have abundant time to fill the order before his busy season comes on. You will be much better satisfied with the rod he makes for you in the winter than if you wait until March before ordering.

If fly lines have been left on the reels, take them off and roll them in coils five inches or more in diameter. If left on the reel a waterproof silk line will come off in small spirals difficult to straighten, and it is a good idea to rub it with a piece of flannel moistened with crude petroleum, then rub this all off, coil loosely and tie coil in three or four places with thread. Hang it up in your tackle cabinet, and now and then during the winter give it a gentle " shaking up," to be sure that it has not gone sticky from too much artificial heat.

A cool closet is the best place for fine lines. It is a good plan to keep a dressed line on one of the large tournament reels, described in Fig. 30. I make it a practice to transfer my line from my fishing reel to a tournament reel as soon as I return from a fishing excursion, and by so doing never have any trouble with the line.

About all that can be done to preserve the braided silk bait-casting line is to keep it dry. The angler has a choice of three kinds: undressed silk; waterproofed silk; and soft dressed. Nearly all treated lines are more difficult to use on a bait reel than those that are not treated, as such lines are more or less wiry, and sometimes spring off the reel in spirals, or cause backlashes. The soft dressed line, being braided softer and finished by hand rubbing, gives less trouble than other lines. Among the better class of undressed lines, the favorites seem to be those that are braided very hard over a heavy, twisted silk core, the braid being so tight as to render the line practically waterproof, or at least against soaking. These lines are also very smooth and keep their shape, which a soft line will not do.

Paraffin dissolved in turpentine and applied quite warm by soaking the line in it will improve undressed silk lines without rendering them wiry, but this, like a paraffin-benzine dressing, will wear off in time. The gossamer-like casting lines have so little body that it is difficult to fill them with anything that will not quickly wear off.

In Mrs. Marbury's " Favorite Flies " a correspondent makes the claim that small casting lines can be improved by soaking them in a warmed solution of paraffin and benzine. He calls this semi-waterproofing and claims that a line so treated will last longer and cast further than any other. The line is not taken out of the solution until the latter cools, in order that all the wax possible may be retained in the line. Dry for a day, then rub with a cloth and chamois skin. I prefer turpentine to benzine, as the former renders the line soft and waxy. The tents which I have treated in this way for many years seem never to rot, are soft and light, and have never leaked.

If you have never used a line dryer, begin now. There are several good and inexpensive ones on the market. No bait line can be depended on if left on the reel over night without drying. A silk line costs from one to four dollars for one hundred yards, and no angler can afford to let a good line rot for want of drying. Lines are frequently injured by minerals in the water they are used in, and if they are dried after use, this may partially offset the harm. If you have no dryer, pull the line off the reel and into your hat, or in a pan, if you are in camp, putting the receptacle in some place where it will not be turned over. In the morning wind the line back on the reel. Never dry a silk line in the sun. A dryer is best, for the line can be left on one over night, so that the air will have abundant time to dry the line thoroughly.

In what shape do you keep your loose hooks, sinkers, swivels, trolling and casting spoons, artificial minnows, etc. ? The neat little boxes these come in are all right, but if one has many, they are bulky enough to fill a suit-case instead of a tackle-box. It is a good plan to put in the tackle-box the reels, lines, etc., customarily taken on fishing trips, then fill in the remaining space with the sliding-top boxes the baits come in. Put away all boxes not needed, and put several baits in each box retained. Each variety in a separate box will simplify matters. The small spinners and casting spoons go nicely into little envelopes to be tucked in corners of the tackle-box, loose hooks in other envelopes, snelled hooks in a box by themselves. A small tin tobacco-box is handy for odds and ends like sinkers, swivels, small spool of silk, wax, and cement.

The trade supplies celluloid and other cases of various shapes for artificial lures, and these are cheap. Lures kept in them are free from rust, arid better still, from the tangling that is inevitable when many devices with hooks attached are kept together. Besides, one may see what is in each envelope without opening it—an immense advantage when he is in a hurry to change lures.

A file, a small bottle of the best reel oil, or better, one of the metal oil tubes; two pairs of small pliers, one with flat, the other with round jaws; and a screwdriver (for reels) should be in every tackle-box. With this equipment you have a complete repair kit, and can change baits to suit conditions as you find them, ashore or afloat.

An assortment of eyed flies is handy, too, for the bait-caster. When bass are taking feathered spinners or spoons, changing flies is often advisable, and this is especially true when single-hook lures are used instead of the now too common trebles. Some anglers remove all treble hooks from artificial lures, replacing them with single bare or feathered hooks, these to be changed to suit conditions. If this practice is followed, it is handy to keep a few lures unmounted, attaching a bare hook and a minnow, or an eyed bass fly, as required. In this connection it is worth noting that few of our hooks of O/O size and thereabout have eyes large enough to go on the wires with which the majority of our spoons and wooden minnows are fitted, necessitating the use of steel split-rings to attach eyed hooks to the lures in a proper manner.

It is a moot question whether treble and groups of treble hooks are worth the trouble and profanity they cause. Some anglers have decided views on this subject, declaring that they can take as many bass on single as on treble hooks. Certainly the single hook is the more sportsmanlike of the two, and I believe the custom of using three to five trebles will give place to the single hook, or at most three singles.

While the lure which carries a single tail-hook is the neatest and least troublesome in weedy waters, for bass it is not always a successful one, because of their habit of striking a bait amidships. Two side hooks and one tail-hook, however, are enough for all practical purposes. It is claimed that pike were responsible for the first trebles and it is also said the devil invented the device. Be that as it may, trebles are put on nearly all lures because such articles are made for jobbers. The retailers are not par-

ticular. They order standard baits, and these are equipped with one, three, or five trebles.

No doubt all manufacturers would be glad to equip their baits with single hooks. Their goods would make a better appearance in sample cases and tackle stores, and _ everybody, from the maker to the angler, could get along without swearing. Trying to put a wooden minnow equipped with treble hooks in a box is like attempting to put a healthy tomcat on his back. When you think you have succeeded, you haven't and afterward you wish you hadn't tried.

Some manufacturers arrange their lures so that the hooks may be changed, just as a fly-fisher changes flies, to suit prevailing conditions. Each spoon or spinner is part of a set, the other members in which consist of four or six eyed flies of well-known merit. I may be prejudiced in their favor, but I have found them valuable additions to my tackle because they are killers, and the flies are well made. Every dealer stocks them.

Many wooden minnows, spoons, and spinners are equipped with feathered treble hooks, the feathers on which are red and white. If bass do not take a fancy to them, the angler often thinks there is something wrong with the lure's size and color when the fault lies in the rooster-feathered hooks. A trial of a few lures fitted with royal coachman, Parmacheene Belle, gray drake, Seth Green, *grizzly* king, buck-tail, silver doctor, or some of the hackles, on single hooks, may alter one's views and give his single-hook lure a wider range of usefulness.

If one fly-fishes often, of course his outfit will be much smaller than if he fishes with both fly-and bait-rods, but if he goes far afield on vacations, he will hardly feel safe without a modest tackle box or book, with a few compact articles tucked away in it. This outfit is a good deal like the emergency medicine case—it may not seem to be worth taking along, but when it is needed, it is needed badly.

It is true that the less one investigates the mechanism of his reel, the better service will it render; but this is not a hard and fast rule. If you do take your reel apart, however, use a screw-driver adapted to that particular purpose. The best type that I have ever seen is obtainable from tackle dealers generally and stores that make a specialty of fine tools. The blade should fit the screwhead slots perfectly, as otherwise they will be marred and will cut the delicate line. The kind referred to has a milled stem fitted with a swivel top that fits in the palm of the hand, so that the driver is held steadily while the fingers alone turn the blade. Such a tool costs a few cents 'more than the common kind, but is invaluable.

Keep a very fine file in the tacklebox. The kind known in the trade as a needle file is best for the purpose. The stem is round, the blade flat on one side and slightly rounded on the other, tapering to a fine point. It is somewhat delicate, but nicely tempered, and will not break if handled with ordinary care. With one of these files the barbs of hooks may be sharpened when they are dull, and so keen is the edge of the file that you can cut through brass and copper wire as with a delicate saw, and small repairs call for a file of this sort.

Rough places on guides, reel-seats or ferrules may be smoothed without scratching the polished surface, though it is well to finish up with a tiny piece of the finest grade of crocus cloth, to insure a good polish. Powdered tripoli, used by machinists for buffing, etc., is also excellent for polishing. Oil a piece of chamois skin, then coat it lightly with tripoli, and you have a good hand polisher for rusted hooks, tarnished trolling spoons, rod fittings, and reels. The tripoli will polish without scratching, but for obstinate cases flour emery in oil may be used. Dry emery cuts too rapidly for any polished surface. Powdered chalk is another good medium for polishing metal. Use crude petroleum with it, and also with tripoli. Crude oil cleans and is a very handy thing to have in the tackle-box. Keep it in one of the little metal tubes previously referred to.

CHAPTER III CARE OF THE RODS WHEN you come to the fishing rods, it is a good plan to take them all out of the tackle cabinet or place where they are kept, joint them up and examine them in a superficial way to see if any ferrules are loose, and if there are any kinks in tops that may be straightened out before the angling season comes around. Too often anglers get into the habit of standing rod-joints in a corner in a closet. If they are protected by wood forms, leather cases, aluminum or bamboo tubes, there is little danger that tips and joints will go crooked, but if left in cloth cases, tied with tapes, they may need straightening. It is handy to keep a rod in a cloth case, but often one tape is tied more securely than others, and the swell of the hand-grasp will help to curve the tips if the rod is left in a dry place for several weeks. The beauty of a fine trout rod may be marred in a short time merely by leaning the joints against a wall.

A better plan is to suspend all the parts from brass brads driven in the walls of the tackle cabinet. The top-rings of the tips will fit these brads, as also the top guides of the joints. Better still, suspend the jointed rod from a hook placed in the ceiling of a cool closet. This applies to split bamboo as well as wood rods, for while the latter are more easily put out of shape during the frequent changes in temperature in winter, split bamboo may also lose its shape in time under the conditions named, particularly the slender tips and middle joints.

If a wood rod becomes hopelessly set through long use and heavy strain, suspend it from a brad driven into the picture moulding in a.cool room, where it will not touch anything, and leave a heavy reel on it, the latter, of course, covered with its chamois bag to keep out dust. After a few damp days you will-notice the change, and before the fishing season opens the rod should be free from set. But if not, hang a weight on the butt in lieu of the reel. Rods used in tournament casting often become set in the direction of the greatest strain, and this is difficult to correct, but the treatment referred to above will help. Applying heat direct, bending in the opposite direction, and leaving the tip under weights are all too severe for a favorite rod, but it should be straightened if this can be done without injuring it, for one cannot cast accurately with a crooked rod.

Another good plan is to fasten the crooked tip or joint to a steel rod or to the edge of a board that is straight. Wind over all with tape or soft cord, being certain that the tip lies true with the axis of the rod.

If you happen to know a metal worker who has an enamelling oven, ask permission to " warm over " your rod in it. A temperature of 150 degrees F. will not harm it if the parts are laid flat on one of the shelves or trays. Straighten the joints as soon as they are taken out of the oven, then suspend them until they are cold. An old split bamboo rod that has lost its " ginger " may be improved by this treatment, as the glue will be warmed slightly, and will set again as the cane cools. The temperature mentioned above will not affect the varnish on the rod, but it is not well to go above that point.

With the rods all jointed up and in shape to be examined and tried for faults, decide on what changes or repairs, if any, should be made by their maker, and do not delay placing such rods in his hand at once, if they require his expert skill. Rodmakers are human and therefore likely to be less thorough when, rushed half to death with hurry orders the week before the fishing season opens than if permitted to take their own time on repair work. You have a right to expect them to do their best work on your rods, but too often you give them very short notice. Be fair to them.

When you have laid aside the rod or rods requiring the repairs that may be made at home, take up one that merely needs cleaning and brightening up. The cork grasp, if soiled and discolored, may be improved by rubbing with a moist cloth and soap. Generally this will suffice to remove the combined oil and dust and leave the cork bright and fresh, but if not, try alcohol on a cloth, turpentine, or even benzine, rubbing the grasp lengthwise to prevent the liquid from softening the glue. After the grasp has dried, roll a piece of tissue paper around it and bind with a couple of elastics, to keep it clean while you work on other parts of the joint. If the grasp be very badly soiled, rub it slightly with an old, worn piece of the finest grade of sand-paper.

Now look over the ferrules. If one is loose, remove it. If it is fastened with a pin, and this does not go clear th'rough, tapping around the pin with the wood handle of a screw-driver may raise it enough so that it may be drawn out with pliers; otherwise, tap lightly with a pointed instrument until the pin is driven below the surface of the ferrule, which may then be removed and the pin drawn from the wood. The best ferrules are pinned through from side to side, and the pins are easily pushed down far enough to be removed with pliers.

Scrape the old cement off the wood, and heating your stick of cement, preferably over the flame of an alcohol lamp, at the same time warming the surface to be coated, spread the cement over the wood and smooth it around with a toothpick. Warm the ferrule just enough to soften the cement that is in it and push it home. It is not difficult to fit it exactly as it was before if a needle be used to locate the hole from which you drew the pin and of course this is desirable, since the making of a new hole may serve to weaken the wood at that point. If any cement exudes below the ferrule, scrape this off with a toothpick, but wait until it is cold before rubbing off all traces of cement with crude oil on a bit of silk or linen. If the ferrule fits the wood too loosely, wind the latter with very thin silk before coating with cement.

Agate guides that are loose in their mountings may be tightened with a tiny drop of cement applied while hot on a toothpick. Do not heat the agate, as it may crack.

Every rodmaker has a. cement of his own and neither sells it nor discloses its ingredients, but when all is said on this subject, there are few cements that will hold longer than shellac. Take a jar of orange shellac that is old and sticky.

Moisten with a few drops of alcohol until it resembles molasses candy. Warm, apply, and be happy.

Take up a rod that has frayed or loose windings here and there; remove all of these and prepare to renew them. Tackle dealers will supply you with winding silk. The colors most used are pale red, black, grass green, and jasper (mottled black and white or brown and white). With the exception of black, all silk darkens when varnished, hence no matter what color you select, see that it is one or two shades lighter than your first choice. Avoid lilac, purple and other delicate shades, as they will fade on being exposed to the sunlight. Orange is a good color, and if you desire less of the so-called barber-pole effect, select cream-colored silk, which is practically transparent under the varnish. Lemon is another shade that gives a nice effect under varnish.

If you must depend on dry goods shops for silk, A is usually the smallest size obtainable, and it will answer, although it is too coarse for nice winding. The larger the rod, the coarser may the silk be, and for salmon and salt water rods I have used button-hole silk for guide and ferrule windings. For trout rods OO is the best size for all windings.

When all of the frayed windings have been renewed, coat the silk, and it alone, with the best grain alcohol shellac, and while this is fresh, pass it over a thin flame, turning the rod rapidly meanwhile. This will cement the windings and the shellac, and make a neat finish. Give the windings a second coat of shellac, and when this is dry, cover the windings with coach varnish, using a fine-pointed brush and letting the varnish extend a trifle beyond the winding on either side.

If guides must be rewound, fasten them in place temporarily with waxed thread and begin to wind with silk toward the guide, not away from it. In this way the end of guide-seat is covered first and the windings will be even, whereas if you begin next the guide and wind away from it, the silk will slip off the end of the guide-seat. Where the guide is to be wound with two or more

colors, as red with green edgings, the two outside edgings should be put on first, and the original silk-end left without cutting, in order that the wider center winding will grip it and hold all together. Both outer edgings being finished, wind the two wide bands, then the two inner edgings.

CHAPTER IV

Cleaning And Varnishing IF the butt-cap and reel-seat of your rod are tarnished, rub them with tripoli on a cloth moistened with crude oil, then polish all of the ferrules in the same manner until they are free from the season's stains. Hold the joint under your left arm, with the ferrule resting on the edge of a table, and polish with a narrow strip of cloth in the same way that a bootblack " shines " your boots. This will leave the metal a dead white that will not glisten in the sun. If there is any varnish on the ferrules, it may be removed with crude oil, but in rubbing be careful not to damage the windings.

Holding the rod as described above, go over it from end to end with just a trace of crude oil on a cloth. Rubbing lengthwise will tend to work the oil into the windings and darken them, whereas all that is needed is to clean and polish the varnish. Some anglers prefer sweet oil for this purpose, but lubricating oils are too penetrating.

Follow with chamois skin or an old silk handkerchief, rubbing briskly, but very lightly, working backward and forward rapidly to avoid heating the varnish through friction.

When the rod is perfectly dry examine it in several places with a microscope. If the varnish is cracked, as it may be after several seasons' use, covering this old varnish with a fresh coat is scarcely to be recommended, when the obvious need is to scrape the rod, rewind, and varnish afresh; but if the varnish is in fair condition, give the rod a new coating. For this purpose buy a three-quarter-inch oval camel-hair brush and a small can of extra light coach varnish. The dealers supply this or equally good rod varnish in small bottles. Do not let anyone persuade you to use shellac.

Before varnishing, leave the rod in a warm room until it is in condition to insure the varnish taking hold, and at the same time put the varnish bottle in a pan of warm water. Coach varnish is quite thick and somewhat gummy. Warming it softens the gum it carries, and makes it flow and set nicely, insuring a more brilliant coating than is possible if it is used cold. Cold varnish may contain minute lumps of gum that amalgamate with the oil when warmed; therefore, use warm varnish.

Coat the winding next to the ferrule first, carefully avoiding the metal. Lay the varnish lightly around each winding, then flow it a trifle more thickly lengthwise of the joint, turning the latter slowly to insure an even coating. This varnish is laid on quite thickly, but not so much so that it will crawl or set in patches. If in doubt, go over the work without any fresh varnish in the brush, touching the varnish very lightly, to smooth it evenly throughout.

Stand each joint in a warm place out of the wind or any draft that may carry dust. When the rod is finished, joint it up and suspend from a hook in a place where no person or object will touch it. It will dry in a few hours, but should not be handled for at least three days. Drying in the sun, while not always harmful, is likely to expose the varnish to dust. Choose a dry day for the work.

Clean the varnish brush carefully with soap and hot water, and when it is dry, put it away in a place free from dust. Keep the varnish bottle tightly corked, and expose the varnish as little as possible to the air.

There is nothing more discouraging to the angler than a failure in varnishing a rod. And varnishing is a delicate operation. One may finish the rod with the utmost care, polishing the wood until it glistens, winding neatly, and then, when it is almost ready for use, have bad luck in varnishing, and feel like throwing the rod away, for apparently it is ruined, and there is nothing left to do but remove windings and guides, scrape it down and begin the work all over again.

This, however, is a mistake, for the fault may be remedied if one is careful.

Take a bethabara rod, for example. This wood is more or less oily. You may finish a rod with the greatest care, wetting the wood to raise the grain, then cutting down all roughness, polishing with mild abrasives, then with fine bethabara shavings, and finally with tissue paper, until the wood glistens like polished brass; but in the winding the natural oil from your hands will coat the wood evenly, and it may not occur to you that the rod is in bad shape for varnishing.

At best bethabara will not absorb much varnish; therefore, it is essential that the varnish shall dry rapidly and not crawl, or solidify in uneven patches, leaving other spots dry. If you varnish the rod on a warm day, turning it round now and then, so that it will dry evenly in the open air, it will be satisfactory; but if circumstances force you to varnish it hurriedly and then hang it up close to a wall, it may dry on one side, while on the other, nearest the wall, the varnish may crawl. This may happen if the temperature is low or the air damp.

When the windings are finished and given two coats of shellac, to preserve the color of the silk, the exposed wood may be rubbed with a strip of linen or silk until most of the oil from your hands has been removed. After this, do not touch the wood with your hands until after the rod has been varnished. Rub the wood lightly, else friction will damage the windings.

Possibly you may forget how old your varnish is, or neglect to have the rod and the varnish warm, or the day selected may turn cold, with the result that the varnish may dry unevenly, remain tacky, or even crawl in places. Old coach varnish may be thinned by adding a little turpentine, then let it stand for a while before using. It is better, however, to buy fresh varnish, particularly as a small bottle or can will furnish enough for several rods. Always apply varnish while warm.

If the varnish does crawl, or fail to dry after several days' time, so that all of your work seems to have been wasted, take a narrow strip of canvas, which has a rough surface and will not shed much lint while you are rubbing, and

wetting it slightly with crude oil, work the strip between the windings as previously described, but never lengthwise of the joint. Very little pressure is needed, for your object will be to warm the sticky varnish through friction, spread it evenly and bind it, while removing a little from the surface. Passing the palm of the hand over the joint occasionally will enable you to tell when the work is finished, which will be when the tacky surface gives way to one that is smooth and fairly hard. Any doubt will be dispelled if you will rub the joint lengthwise very lightly with a piece of linen or silk. If this sticks in places, those spots must be polished.

Let the rod stand for a day, then pass the dry silk strip over it lightly, and if all parts are hard, polish with this strip. The high gloss will be gone, but if a thin coat of varnish is put on in a few days, this should bring out all of the beauty of the grain and the windings, and your rod, which seemed to be ruined, will be little the worse for this heroic—and perhaps unworkmanlike—treatment. We are not all experts, and few of those who love to " tinker at rod building" have just the right sort of workshops and tools, but a little horse sense has saved more valuable property than a fishing rod.

Now and then the claim is made that vaseline is a preservative that should be used on the rod before it is put away for the winter. Vaseline would very likely keep out dampness, but it is very penetrating, and if there are cracks in the varnish, the vaseline would work into them, and discolor windings as well. It seems to me that crude petroleum is a better preservative, but if it is used it should be completely removed before varnishing. Verdigris will form on brass coated with vaseline, and the same thing applies, though in a lesser degree, to German silver, hence this seems to me to be another argument against the use or vaseline on rods.

Lard oil should be better. I have never used it to prevent fishing rod ferrules from sticking, but have found it peculiarly effective when applied to the friction joints of canoe paddles and tent poles, and see no reason why it should not work well on fishing rods. It is a clean oil, and a very little of it goes a long way. Common lubricating oil, and vaseline as well, pick up grit, and the combination is likely to injure ferrules. All of the lubricating that a good ferrule needs is to wipe it clean, then rub it over youf hair if it fits too snugly.

CHAPTER V REELS AND THEIR CARE GENERALLY speaking, there are but two kinds of reel used in fresh water fishing: (i) the single-action reel for fly-rods, and (2) the multiplying reel for bait (*Courtesy of Wm. Mills & Son.*) Fig. I.—Rubber and German Silver Single Action ReeL (*Courtesy of Wm. Mills & Son.*)

Fig. 2.—Light Click Reel.

In fishing with the fly-rod the reel is employed mainly in playing a fish and in shortening line. In casting the fly or lure the actual length of line is controlled by the left hand. With it the line is pulled off the reel or stripped in, to be held in one or more coils, and to be wound up on the reel when it is necessary to shorten line. But when a fish is hooked the reel comes into play when there is too much line out to control it by rod manipulation alone.

This being true, there are only a few things to consider in selecting a reel. It should balance nicely on the rod and be no larger than is necessary to hold the line. Weight is a matter each angler must decide for himself. One prefers a fairly heavy reel, claiming that it balances the rod; another selects a light reel because it does not place too much weight below the hand.

A single-action reel need not be expensive. The parts should be well made and nicely fitted, the click one that will not get out of order quickly, and with a good strong spring. The click must be just strong enough to prevent the spool from turning when casts of ordinary length are made without holding the line with either hand. The reels illustrated in Figs. I and 2 are typical of the moderate priced reels used by trout fishermen. Three inches is the diameter of most click reels on which thirty yards of double tapered E line are used, and they will carry the same length of D line if it be

wound on evenly. There is no need of a drag on a fly reel.

The English reels are nearly all heavy affairs, but they are beautifully made and compact. Nearly all are so made that by removing one screw the spool may be taken out, and instead of the thin axle—which ruins any line left on it for any length of time,—there is a drum of good size. The dry-fly reel shown in Fig. 3 is of this type. It is narrow but of goodly diameter, and light, as the material is an aluminum alloy—aluminum alone being too soft for reels.

Whatever reel is employed, do not leave a (*Courtesy of Wm. Mills & Son.*) Fig. 3.—Narrow Dry-Fly Reel, good line on it, but wind the line on one of the large " reels" used by tournament casters, illustrated in Fig. 30; or wind it on to a line dryer.

Salmon reels are merely larger editions of trout reels, but as they are roughly handled at times, strength is necessary, and for this purpose a high-grade reel is the best.

The bait-casting reel is a machine in miniature and is a wonderful one at that. It must be light and small, run almost as freely as a top, yet withstand tremendous strains and sudden shocks. Nowhere else are such perfect reels made as in the United States, and Kentucky has produced the two that are types. For nearly a century the Milam and the Meek reels have been on the market, and the first reels these firms made are almost identical with the modern ones.

Fig. 4..—Milam No. 2 Quadruple Multiplying Reel. Exact Size.

At a national tournament a few years ago, the winner of the accuracy bait-casting event used a tiny No. i reel that had been used by the owner for many years, and by his father before him; more than fifty years in all, surely. And that reel is as good to-day as a new one and differs from the present-day type only in that it has a crank handle instead of a balanced handle.

Fig. 5.—Meek No. 2 Reel. Three-fourths Actual Size. One improvement that has been made in recent years is in the use of spiral gears instead of the old

straight gears. Spiral gears mesh more smoothly, and the wear is more uniform, while greater strength is attained, as a greater bearing surface between pinion and gear is had. Another improvement is the screw-off cap over each end of the axle. This makes it possible to oil these main bearings without taking the reel apart. Garnets are fitted in these bearings if desired, insuring longer wear than is possible with the customary steel bearings.

A satisfactory fishing reel may be had for $5 or a little less, but it is good economy to pay $15 for a far better reel, and if you can afford the very best, $25 to $30. Such a reel will outlast your fishing days, and always be dependable. The old-time free running reel has no superior; by " free running " is meant that there is no graduated device for retarding the speed of the spool. Free-spool reels are of another class, in which there is a device to throw the gears out of mesh during a cast, the handle remaining at rest, the gears engaging while the line is being wound in. They are excellent reels, but considerable practice is necessary to cast without backlashing, as the spool-action is very rapid.

Fig. 6.—Meek No. 3 Blue Grass Reel. If you ask a manufacturer how to take one of his reels apart for cleaning, he will probably tell you not to attempt this at all, as only " one skilled in the art," as inventors say, can adjust a reel properly. This is of course true of some reels in the hands of careless persons, but one who possesses ordinary skill may easily take apart, clean, oil, and reassemble a reel without injuring it in the least. There is no other course left open to one who happens to be far from repair shops when his reel needs attention, and the sooner he learns how to care for it himself, the better off will he be.

If your reel has oil-caps, by removing these and the handle, you can oil the end bearings, the pinion, and the handle and gear-post without disturbing the adjustment of the parts. This is an immense advantage, but all bearings should be cleaned before oiling.

In reels that have capped face plates

this is a simple matter, as the screws merely hold the cap in place and exert uniform pressure on the spindle ends, and one may take out the gear, clean its post and teeth, the pinion and all bearings, replace the cap by means of three or four screws, none of which enter the pillars. All bearings save one may be cleaned without disturbing the adjustment of the frame. In order to get at this one, the face plate of some but not all reels must be removed and the spool taken out. Some reels are easy to readjust because the front plate is held by only one, or at most four screws; but those that have a screw in each one of the five pillars must be readjusted with the utmost care, and patience is necessary, as you must set the screws, test it, and perhaps repeat this two or three times before all is well.

The cap screws should be turned down easily and the spool tried, to see if there is any play longitudinally. Some reels require a little play, while others do not.

Before touching a screw try the spool and ascertain how much play it has. Then lay your watch in front of you, and holding the reel in the left hand with the handle up, so that the handle and gears will revolve horizontally, grasp the handle with the thumb and first two fingers of the right hand, the second finger on the handle-knob, and spin the reel smartly as the second hand of your watch passes a certain point, noting how long it takes for the handle to lose all motion. Try this three or four times until you are certain that the spool will spin just so long each time. If there is a line on the reel, tuck its ends under with a toothpick, to prevent it from striking the pillars and retarding the spool.

In turning the cap screws down, test the spool for play and speed, bearing in mind that since cleaning and oiling all bearings it should spin several seconds longer than when foul with gummed oil—that is, unless you have put too much oil on gear and pinion, in which case the reel may be out of commission until the surplus oil is removed. If ten seconds was the time of spinning while dirty, fourteen or fifteen seconds should

be about right for the clean spool, and if it falls below this, tighten the screws a trifle more and try again for time and play. If all screws are tightened uniformly, a few trials will show you when to stop, and if these directions are religiously followed, the reel should be in perfect order.

It is important that a good screw-driver and the best reel oil be used. It is also advisable to examine all bearings, after cleaning, with a microscope, at the same time removing all particles of grit or dust with the end of a toothpick. The pinion in a good reel is made from tool steel, and the gear from bronze or hard brass, but a tiny speck of grit is a bad thing for either one.

All tests should be made while the spool of the reel is filled with the line that you are accustomed to using in fishing practice. Exerting equal force, the spool will spin one-fourth to one-third longer when filled with line than when empty.

In these remarks quadruple multiplying reels are referred to, for the reason that nearly all of the small fishing and all of the tournament reels are geared thus. No properly made quadruple reel has four times as many teeth in the gear as in the pinion. Generally there are three or four teeth less in the gear, the number depending largely on the diameter decided on for that wheel as the best when the diameter of plates, length of spool and handle, and general purpose of reel are taken into consideration. One good reason for the odd number of teeth in the large gear is that every tooth in the pinion bears on every one in the gear, always changing, and in this way the wear is equalized and the meshing is perfect at all points in every revolution.

Every tooth added to the large gear decreases the strength and winding power of the mechanism, and the logical conclusion is that the double multiplier is best for reels of large size, where power is preferred to speed in delivering and recovering line. This is illustrated in eighty-yard quadruple reels used for bass fishing and tournament casting. The spool of the fishing reel may be i%

inches in length and $4 inches in diameter, with a balance handle 2j4 or 2/2 inches in length. The spool of the tournament reel may be I 4 inches long, i inches in diameter, very thin and light, and the handle only I ⅞ inches long. The latter will spool thin line beautifully and deliver it rapidly, but if used in fishing it will recover line very slowly when a two-pound bass is tugging at the hook, the small spool and the short handle furnishing very little leverage.

On the other hand, the fishing reel will handle large bass easily, but when used in tournament casting, it will be found that the handle is too long and the spool too narrow and deep for nice, even spooling and delivery. The reel that is a modification of both types referred to will give fair satisfaction at the tournament and on the lake, and for the man of one outfit this is the reel to own.

Some anglers prefer to let German silver reels tarnish—as they will in fresh water impregnated with mineral substances, and from contact with one's hands—but others do not. It is true that this tarnishing takes the place of the glitter of the freshly buffed reel, although German silver glistens far less than the nickle of cheap reels; but it is one thing to let the reel tarnish slightly, and quite another to permit dust and gummed oil to accumulate until the usefulness of the reel is affected. The reel should be cleaned thoroughly at least once each season, preferably in the winter.

The easiest way to polish the frame is with a buffer, but chamois skin and tripoli will remove all harmful dirt from smooth surfaces, while the angles may be reached by folding the leather over a sliver of soft pine and rubbing with this. The bearings must not be touched with any abrasive or polishing substance. They should be cleaned thoroughly with benzine—but do not light your pipe during this operation. An old soft toothbrush and benzine should be used on pinion, gear, and all bearings, and in order to be sure that the parts are cleared from gummed oil, examine them when they are dry under a microscope.

This inspection should be minute. A

good reel is to a certain extent a delicate machine, and although you may not remember it, it may be that you dropped rod and reel at some time last summer while fishing and damaged the gears. Perhaps you have wondered why its song has a harsh note, but still it seems to be all right. If any of the bearings show wear in places where they should be smooth, or if the teeth of pinion or gear have any rough spots— under the glass these teeth resemble those in a huge saw—send the reel post haste to its maker. He alone can put it to rights. Otherwise, when all the parts are absolutely clean, put the reel together again, using the second hand of your watch to determine its correct adjustment, as previously described. Every reel should be kept in a chamois bag or in one of the chamois-lined sole leather cases. Then put it away in the tackle-box, making a mental note to oil it slightly the night before you go away on your first fishing trip next spring.

Beginners may fail to notice an important point in connection with the timing of the reel for adjustment by the watch. The present-day quadruple multiplying reels—most of them, at least— will spin longer when the spool is horizontal than otherwise, but this is not a fair test, as in casting with the short rod the hand is turned to the left—(i) to insure the line running through the guides and top without fouling the rod; and (2) because there is less friction on the bearings of the reel when it is held handle up (Fig. 7). In timing his reel the novice will naturally turn the balance handle from left to right, and if it spins say twenty-one seconds, he will put that down as its time and never stop to consider the fact that he is turning it backward, or in the direction the handle turns when the spool is taking up the line—where smoothness and speed do not so much count,

Another thing: if his reel has spiral gears, as many of the best reels have, its spool may not revolve so freely in recovering as in delivering, therefore one will not gain a fair knowledge of its capabilities for casting unless he spins it backward. This is more difficult to do

with thumb and finger because of the form of the balance handle.

A better plan, and one giving more accurate results is this: Take a piece of small cord and wax one end. Lay this on the spindle of the spool and wind over it, just as you would with a casting line, always winding a given length of cord, say twelve inches. Hold the reel firmly in one hand, handle at the top, and when the second hand of your watch is over a given point, pull the cord evenly with the other hand until it comes away from the spindle—just as a boy spins a top. Pull steadily, exerting not much more force than would the half-ounce weight in a cast. Your reel will spin as it does in casting, and the method insures steadiness and uniform results, as you will find after a few trials.

If the reel is made of hard rubber with bronze or brass parts, on taking it apart you may find verdigris under and in the teeth of the gear, and this, as well as the gummed oil, must be cleared out. A good reel is a constant source of pride to its owner, if he appreciates it, and while few other mechanical " contrivances " are called upon to and do withstand so many severe shocks and strains, a little grit in its vitals will cause as much trouble to it as a small pebble in your shoe will to you. Neither one is fatal, but may have a bad effect in time.

The gears and pinions of various reels differ slightly. Some mesh closely, the leaves of the pinion fitting rather tightly in the teeth of the gear. These require rather thin oil, but do not use any of the thin bicycle oils, some of which contain substances of no value to reels. Ask your dealer for the best reel oil, or obtain a bottle of oil from a watchmaker. If properly used, an ounce of reel oil will last several seasons. It must be applied sparingly, and only on clean parts. Generally, but not invariably, the larger the reel the heavier may the oil be, and some salt water reels work well if petroleum jelly or graphite is applied to the gears, though nothing but the best oil should be put on smooth bearings.

If, when the oil is applied, the reel seems to be jammed and will not spin freely, it is a good sign that the gears

are gummed up, or that too much or too heavy oil has been applied. Clean thoroughly and try again with less oil. It is possible to completely clog the mechanism of a fine reel with oil, and reels are often sent back to their makers as " no good," when the only fault is that too much oil has been put in them. In a quadruple reel of high grade, whose gears mesh closely, a drop too much may completely stop the turning of the parts. CHAPTER VI CORK DRUMS FOR REELS IT is customary for anglers to use a reel larger than they need, and to fill the spool one-third to one-half full of old or common line, then wind on the line that is to be used in fishing. When it is ready to use, the spool is two-thirds or three-fourths filled, enabling one to thumb it more readily, and as its size increases through wetting, one turn of the spool releases or recovers much more line than if the winding of the good line were begun on the empty spool.

There are some objections to this plan, particularly as applied to the small long-spool reels used in bait-casting contests and in fishing. If the dummy is composed of coarse line, it is difficult to spool it evenly, leaving an uneven surface on which the fine casting line must be wound. If common thread is used for a dummy, it is difficulty to wind it so that it will be hard and firm. This must be done in order to attain the best results, as a spongy foundation for the gossamer-like casting line will increase the tendency toward backlashing, and it will lose its cylindrical form after repeated casting, causing one's thumb to press hard at one place and skip at another. After use the silk casting line must be wound on a dryer or coiled on a smooth surface until thoroughly dry, and as such a line is generally one hundred yards or more in length, it is a nuisance to take off the dummy, too, but as it gets wet and will not dry on the reel, off it comes or it would ruin the silk line.

If you use a long-spool reel in casting, with a line thinner than H size, you will need a dummy i or ij/s inches in diameter. A good plan is to fit cork disks on the spool. These can be obtained at cork stores. Either vaseline bottle corks or rod grasp corks will serve. Select four perfect corks, and with an old ferrule cut holes through the exact center of each one, concaving the ends of two, so that they will fit the convex spool ends. Take the spool out of the reel while fitting corks. Split all of the corks from the central holes to the rim, using a very thin sharp knife blade.

Obviously the hole in each cork must be a trifle larger than the spindle of the spool, over which the end corks are to be fitted first. After fitting the end corks, slip the third one into place, and while there is room, coat each cork very slightly with shellac. Split the fourth cork so that it will fill the remaining space snugly and slip it on, shellacking the slit in each cork and turning all so that no two slits come opposite each other. Wind a bit of thread over all to hold them in place until dry, then remove the thread and shave off all uneven places.

Smoothing the corks to perfect form should be done in a lathe with a fine file, but if a lathe is not at hand, assemble the reel and fasten it lightly in a vise, the jaws of which are covered with cloth to protect the reel-yoke. Turn the handle with one hand and hold the file with the other, being careful that it does not touch the ends of the spool. Exert the least possible pressure in grinding the cork drum to perfect form, blowing the cork dust away from the reel frequently.

Measure the diameter of the drum, and when it is correct, wind the entire drum with thread, being as careful as if you were winding a fine rod. Pull both ends of the thread under with a separate loop, and leave the second one to tie the casting line to. Coat this winding twice with shellac, which will bind it and preserve the shape of the drum. Otherwise it may bulge in places. When the shellac is dry, clean the reel and wind the casting line on it. This should fill the spool three-fourths, allowing for a slight increase when the line is wet. The cork being extremely light, the weight of the wet line is placed further away from the axis of the spool, giving the reel increased efficiency in casting.

For a reel the diameter of which is two inches and the length of the spool i J4 inches, the cork dummy should be i or I 1/16 inches in diameter for a tournament line, and this should be sufficient for the fishing reel, which requires less diameter of wound line than does the tournament line.

The simplest way to determine the diameter for the cork dummy is this: wind the fine casting line on the bare spindle, and on this wind common thread until the spool is three-fourthsi filled. Cut the thread and remove it from the reel; remove the casting line and replace the thread on the reel. Measure its mean diameter, which will be correct for the dummy.

Generally speaking, one can safely place more line on a tournament than on a fishing reel, as he watches the line carefully while spooling it in tournament work, but may not do so while playing a fish, and if he is careless the line may foul the pillars and a sudden jerk by the fish may break the line.

If there are to be changes in lines, the diameter of the cork should be reduced slightly, and a dummy line employed to make up the re-required diameter when the reel is full. The cork is firm and even but not hard, and the device is a useful one. Nearly all tournament casters employ cork dummies, and a few reels have been made with metal drums, which are of course more substantial than cork. It is a pity that more standard reels are not made with metal drums.

CHAPTER VII LEADERS, GUT, AND EYED FLIES THE production of silkworm gut has not kept pace with the demand, which has increased enormously during the last quarter century.

The best silkworm gut comes from Spain, the market being practically controlled by British firms. The high price of gut has created a demand for substitutes, but while there are several of these, as a general thing they are unsatisfactory. There is no doubt that a good substitute will be produced in time, but in order to be a success it must be less flabby and soft, when wet, than the present substitutes. These are very strong, but after a little soaking they become stringy and soft, and are of little value for fly casting. The one advantage they possess is that they are made without knots. A tapered leader can be made of this stuff with only two or three knots.

As silkworm gut is drawn, the larger or salmon sizes average nine or ten inches in length, while the bass sizes are twelve to fourteen inches long, and the trout sizes up to eighteen or twenty inches. With every strand there is considerable waste. They are put up 100 in a hank, and are generally sold by the trade in this shape, though retailers sometimes put them up in lots of twenty-five, so that anglers who make their own leaders can obtain an assortment of three or four sizes—enough to make several tapered leaders—without purchasing several hanks of 100 strands each.

In recent years the demand for bleached and stained gut has decreased steadily. Perhaps gut was at first bleached because in that shape it shows to better advantage than the natural article. The staining was for the purpose of rendering it less conspicuous in the water, but experience has proved that neutral colors are not of so much importance as they were at one time popularly believed to be; witness the various lines, in which white and black and showy colors are all successfully used in taking fish.

Bleaching injures the gut. Staining does or does not; it depends on the agent employed. Soaking in cold tea, rubbing with dock leaves, and a number of other harmless things have long been used in dulling the gloss of new gut without injuring it.

The names given the various sizes of Spanish silkworm gut, and their calibers, in thousandths of an inch, follow: Leaders commonly used for trout fishing are not expensive, as they are small in size and composed of the longest strands; but tapered leaders, now used for dry-fly fishing, cost more. The tapered salmon leaders, which are made up from three or four of the heaviest sizes of gut, retail at $3 to $6 each. In a nine-foot leader of this sort there are many short strands, and these short strands must be selected with the greatest care, because so many more of them are imperfect than in the smaller sizes.

Salmon leaders are sometimes made with the upper third of three strands of small gut, twisted hard; the middle of two strands, twisted; and the point of medium weight single gut. In the twisted gut the ends are sometimes knotted separately, or the strands are spliced, while the double gut strands are knotted in pairs. Nice tapers are obtained in this way, but after soaking the twisted gut swells more than the single gut, and is not so smooth and wiry, though strong.

In olden times horsehair leaders were much used, and are still employed to some extent in England. The hairs from the tail of a gray stallion were said to be the best, while those from a mare's tail were regarded as useless.

In tournament fly-casting for distance the finest grade leaders are used, mainly in salmon sizes. In the salmon events combination leaders are allowed, but for all single-hand rods the leaders must be of single gut. The general rule observed in the United States is that every tournament leader must be at least six feet in length, and it cannot exceed the length of the rod used by more than two feet. In Australia, where tournament casting is practiced by an enthusiastic group of Sydney trout fishermen, leaders of twenty and thirty feet are used, and with their strong, dry winds, this in part accounts for the great distances they have accomplished in casting with heavy single-hand rods.

Formerly leaders of fifteen and eighteen feet were used here in distance casting, but since the casters have all adopted lines with very long tapers, leaders average rather less than the length of the rods. Those used with all rods are much alike. They taper from the heaviest salmon size down to heavy trout size, and are selected with great care, since to whip off a fly means the loss of that cast and an important part of the time alloted the caster. For this use it is better to use a heavy level leader than to have the point too fine. In the accuracy wet-fly contests, in which a short leader is an advantage, the minimum limit of six feet is standard. In the dry-fly accuracy events medium to light weight leaders are used, generally just over six feet in length, and tapered.

The new dry-fly leaders—for fishing—are generally 7 feet long; tapered from medium to very fine trout gut, with one loop, at the line end. As one fly only is employed in this branch of trout fishing, the dropper loops tied in wet-fly leaders are objectionable.

The old-time leaders were three, six, and nine feet in length. But in place of the six and seven ounce rods used with them, four-and-three-quarter ounce tournament rods nine feet in length are now much used in dry-fly fishing. These rods are rather stiff and very powerful, hence in order to develop the best qualities of the rod, it is necessary to use a heavy double tapered line. Size F, the old favorite, is giving way to E, and the D size is also much used.

In these lines the taper is short, 12 feet or less. Thus it will be understood that a 9-foot taper and a 734-foot leader, propelled by a fairly heavy line on a stiff rod, may be depended on in all sorts of weather for accurate casts of fifteen to twenty-five feet. And for long casts this equipment is ideal.

While these rods are excellent for fishing on large streams, on rocky and overgrown woods brooks, three, two, and even ij ounce rods of 7 to 8 *y* feet are favorites with many anglers. Even with these little rods fairly heavy lines are the rule, the short tapers being fine at the ends, so that small 4/2-and 6-foot leaders can be handled accurately at short range.

In working out with the dry-fly—which must be done without touching the water in front—it is much more difficult to handle rod and line in places that are overhung with trees than in wet-fly casting, hence the utility of the heavy line, short taper, and short leader.

It is good fun to make up your own leaders on winter nights. But even if you do not do this, it is economical to repair those that have been used, and put them in good condition for the coming season. Soak them well; it is a good plan to put all leaders to be repaired in a tray of water, taking out each one as needed. Examine the loop, and if it is frayed or broken, cut it off and tie a new one. This is made by doubling the gut, passing the single loop thus formed around the doubled strands and under the double loop, then pulling taut. Fig. 9 shows

Fig. 9.—Forming the Leader Loop. this, but bear in mind that twisting the strands will result in a bad knot. Cut the short end close to the knot. It will not pull out.

Make the loop short, and attach end of line to leader as shown in Fig. 10. This is a

Fig. 10.—Attaching End of Line to Leader simple but very secure fastening, and one which may be untied without difficulty or injury to the line. The end of line may be looped back, so that it may be pulled out readily, but this makes a clumsy knot, and is unnecessary. Another method that is followed by some anglers is to attach a short loop of heavy gut to the end of the line, so that the leader can be looped over this. It is satisfactory if the gut loop be soaked before strain is put on it, and also provided the loop be very firmly made fast. It should be soaked thoroughly, then whipped on with heavily waxed silk under considerable tension, so that it cannot pull out.

Examine all knots in the leader, and if the gut be broken next to one of them—as frequently happens—cut it and tie a new knot. This may at first seem to be a difficult matter, but if you will practice with the ends of a piece of cord large enough to give you a clear idea how the thing is done, it will be easy to master. Many knots are in common use, but with most of them the ends of the gut stick out parallel with the strands, and are rough and untidy. In the knot given in Fig. 11 the ends stand out at right angles to the strands, and may be clipped off close to the knot, as they cannot pull out. The ends of the gut are overlapped slightly, then one end is turned twice around the other strand and secured between the two. Reverse ends and tie the second part of the knot in the

Fig. II.—Method of Tying a Leader Knot.

same way. When pulled taut the ends may be cut off close.

Accidental knots can usually be worked out and the gut straightened, but if not, replace that strand with a new one.

When the new leader is finished, or the old one repaired, suspend it from a brad driven in a picture moulding, and attach a weight to the lower end, to stretch it slightly while it is drying. A dipsy sinker is excellent for this purpose. When dry take the leader down, coil it and put it away in a dry, dark place, with a tag attached, giving its length and size. Gut should never be kept in a strong light.

Finally, swear off using snelled flies and stock up on eyed flies instead. These are better in every way, but one advantage alone is sufficient—you have no snells to soak in changing flies. Besides, the snells are a nuisance in every way. It is almost impossible to keep the fly-book in which they are kept tidy, and it is bulky and awkward to handle on the stream. The neat little aluminum fly-boxes (Figs. 12 and 13) m

Fig. 12.—Eyed Fly-Box with Clips.
Fig. 13.—Eyed Fly-Box with Partitions and Transparent Covers.

are compact, roomy, and on opening one you see at a glance all its contents. And every fly is securely fastened in its proper place.

If it is desired to use eyed wet flies—two or more—these are attached to the leader with short tippets, kept in the leader soak-box when not in use.

Whether the eyed fly is attached to point of leader or to a tippet, the Turle knot (Fig. 14)

C

C/

Fig. 14.—The Turle Knot.

is one of the simplest and best. Pass the gut through the eye of hook and tie a slip knot with a loop large enough to go over the fly without injuring it. Pull the loop tight over head of fly and clip end close.

For cutting gut, removing knots, and handto a knot, but with this clipper the

work is neatly done.

Fig. 15.—Gut Clipper and Tweezer ling small flies, the combination clipper and tweezer (Fig. 15) is highly recommended. With ordinary scissors it is difficult to clip close

In recent years the fishing tackle makers of Great Britain have adopted a new system of numbering hooks. This is called the new scale. Americans, however, adhere to the old system, known as the Redditch scale. Both systems are shown in Fig. 16, the lower figures giving the old or Redditch scale, in common use in the United States, while the upper figures show the new scale.

At the close of the fishing season, put away the fly-book or box in a mothproof receptacle. A red cedar box is the safest place, but a metal box that has a tight-fitting cover will answer. As an additional precaution, put camphor balls or crystals with the flies, but do not sprinkle any of the latter over them, for this may serve to rust the hooks. Still, it is not safe to leave fly-book or box closed, even though camphor is present. Instead, leave it open, so that the fumes of the camphor will penetrate between all leaves. The best plan is to secure a small atomizer, put gasoline in it, and spray all of the flies before putting them away for the season. This, with the camphor, will keep away moths, and destroy any eggs that may already be among the flies.

15 10 IS 17 1C jr, 11 13 12 n 10 9 B 7 6 5 13
I-I

Fig. 16.—Lower Figures Give the Numbers in the Red-ditch Scale. Upper Figures, the New Scale.

Repeat this at least once during the winter, in order to be on the safe side. If you ever open your fly-book on a cold night—just to renew acquaintance with old friends—and find your favorite flies a mass of fluff, you will not need a second warning. Where there are moths the utmost care is necessary in protecting flies.

CHAPTER VIII ROD CASES AND FORMS ON the use to which you will put your rod depends the kind of protective covering you will need. There are anglers

who will have nothing but a thin muslin cover, but something better is needed for rods that are to be carried far.

The makers of the best fly-rods supply aluminum or bamboo tubes with screw caps for the tips, this tube and the middle and butt joint going into a canvas case, so that the stiff tube protects the two other parts when all are bound with the tie-tapes of the cover. The wood form is the most common type, and these are cheap. Aluminum tubes with screw caps are suitable for either fly or bait rods. Aluminum tubing of almost any desired size is obtainable from the supply companies, at 20 to 50 cents per foot, and fiber tubing of similar sizes can be had from some hardwareman at about the same prices. Both fiber and aluminum, tubes are made in sizes up to about two inches. For long rods a tube of some sort is very handy. It can be fitted with corks, or with a screw cap on one end, and in a case of this sort a rod is safe from hard knocks.

Tip cases are sometimes made to order by houses that supply mailing tubes. The method of winding the strips of strawboard spirally makes these tubes tough and strong, and if the walls are thick, the ends corked and the tube supplied with a canvas case, the rod will be well protected. I have seen these tubes as small as one inch in diameter, for long tips. Sometimes they are covered with leather. They are frequently made thus for bait-casting rods which have separate handgrasps, the grasps to be carried in a pocket or tackle case.

A very good plan is to groove a piece of white pine so that the tips of the rod will lie below the surface, the grooves being enlarged to let the guides go underneath, then inclose this form in a canvas case with the butt and joint, the whole rod being fairly well protected. Choose a piece an inch thick and about 2 inches wide.

Still another way is to employ a canvas case of the form illustrated in Figs. 17 and 18. The upper end is bound with braid or is hemmed, the lower edge turned over and sewed length- r

Figs. 17 and 18.—Canvas Case for Rods. wise and three tapes attached to the back. This leaves pockets for the butt, the joint and the two tips. One of the tip pockets is made large enough to admit a piece of wood a half-inch square and of the same length as the tips. Round off its corners and it will not injure the tip. When the rod is taken out of the case this piece of wood will remain to protect the extra tip, which might otherwise be broken.

CHAPTER IX GENERAL HINTS THE creel is usually associated with trout fishing, when, as a matter of fact, it is one of the handiest things the fisher has fallen heir to for all sorts of fishing in which wading or walking is the rule—fishing from a boat, of course, calling for another sort of kit. But there are all sorts of creels. The best one for all-round use is the long, thin creel. It is no more trouble to carry than one of the short, thick kind; in fact, it is less likely to catch on briers, trees, and wire fences as one walks along a stream. If you will improve it to suit your own needs, it will be still more useful. There is space enough in it for a small kit, lunch, and any ordinary number of fish you may catch before noon. But if lunch, fly-box, soak-box, and other articles are all jumbled together in it, it is awkward to put your fish in with them. Remedy this by putting a partition in the creel. Some anglers divide 80 the creel with a piece of fiber or a strip of canvas laced to the bottom and ends; others use insulated wires. Whatever is put in should be immune from damage when the creel is washed out.

If the partition is close to the back of the basket, and extends nearly to the top, this will give you ample space for fly-book, soak-box, and package of lunch. The larger space, in the front of the creel, will then be clear for the fish you catch. The bottom being lower at the front, the water that enters with your catch will drain off without wetting your lunch. With this arrangement every article " stays put."

In my creel I carry a landing-net which collapses, and this reduces the outfit to two parts to be carried—rod and creel. The landing net referred to has a bronze hoop about a foot in diameter—I cut mine down to nine inches. It may be extended or contracted like a spiral clock spring. When closed or open the hoop is clamped rigidly by means of a set-screw. The handle is a short piece of bamboo. In the end of this I put a piece of rawhide four inches long, securing it with a cork shellacked and driven in. The net is of ample size. When closed, the net is wound around the hoop, and in this shape the device is about five inches wide by eleven inches in length. It occupies little space in the back of the creel.

The rawhide strap has a slit ending in an eyelet. On the web shoulder-strap of the creel a metal button is sewed. When the creel is in place this button is just over the left shoulder. The strap is buttoned on and the landing net rests behind the left shoulder. When the net is wanted the strap is within reach of either hand. It is next to impossible to lose a landing net secured in this fashion. It is not in the way of either hand while one is fishing, and when wanted it may be detached in an instant without any fumbling.

When one is wading a stream there is always the possibility that he may slip and fall in swift water. The seriousness of such an accident depends largely on the character of the water and the shore immediately below him and on the clothing and equipment. It being second nature for an angler to cling to his rod through thick and thin, if he is encased in heavy wading trousers and brogues and carries a heavy creel secured with straps and buckles, he may be in for a very unpleasant ten minutes before he gets his feet under him again on solid bottom. At such a time it is foolhardy to think of swimming. Instead, exert every effort to keep your head upstream, and turning face down, so that creel and landing net will drift behind you, stop your progress with hands and feet, gain a foothold, and rise slowly. If it is necessary to free yourself of the creel, this is much more easily done with one hand if the fastenings are snaps instead of buckles.

For use in dry-fly fishing I soldered a rather large safety pin on one of the ten-cent oil tubes sold everywhere by the trade. Filled with paraffin oil, it is pinned on the creel shoulder strap or secured on the leather strap that passes through the back of the creel, where it cannot be turned upside down.

As the screw cap of this tube is a clumsy thing to handle, I improved it, too. A small hole was drilled into its top, then a larger one was bored through it from side to side, tapping the first hole. A piece of silk line was pushed down the hole in the top and out at one side, a knot tied in the end and pulled into the cap. The other end of the cord was tied into the safety pin. As the cord will swivel, the cap may be unscrewed without snarling it, and it cannot be lost.

There are a number of handy devices to be had in the trade for carrying paraffin oil and other solutions intended to make flies float. One of them is a tiny atomizer which is cleaner to use than any bottle or other receptacle, from which oil may find its way into one's clothing, there to remain " for keeps."

For floating a dressed line, use crude petroleum—a drop on a piece of flannel is sufficient to float the heaviest tapered line. It is also excellent for cleaning the line occasionally. Use it sparingly, and wipe the line dry afterward.

For wet weather purchase a fishing shirt. These waterproof shirts, some of them, are big and comfortable to wear, but may be folded into a package not much more bulky than a sou'wester. This head-piece is another handy article to take along on day trips, unless you wear a felt hat, which in itself is more or less waterproof. I have been out all day in a downpour of rain many a time, but, clad in a sou'wester, fishing shirt, and wading trousers, was dry and comfortable.

CHAPTER X EQUIPMENT FOR FLY-AND BAIT-CASTING SO many inquiries have come to me from anglers in relation to fly-and bait-casting practice that a few remarks on the subject may not be out of place here. Not only are clubs being formed now and then, but small groups of anglers in towns and villages wish to practice under tournament conditions, in order that they may compare their work with that of other anglers who are enabled to watch expert casters and obtain advice from them, and to cast under their coaching as well. Club members practice tournament casting in order that they may become better anglers, and in group or club practice the angler attains better results than he can possibly hope for in experimenting alone. The principal fault in practicing alone is that he cannot see the faults that a companion may readily point out, and in this way he may fall into errors very difficult to correct. Friendly criticism is of immense advantage.

Tournament casting is largely a game, but it teaches many useful things. For example, the fly-fisher may supply himself with the finest of tackle, but if he lacks coolness and self-control, he may lose his largest trout by striking too hard or playing it roughly in his impatience: but if he knows exactly how to cast his fly, the strength of his leader, the limitations of his rod, etc., the battle is half won when the trout is hooked, for he feels confident and cool.

On the other hand, no matter how skillful he may be in fly-fishing, let him take part for the first time in a club contest, and his stream-acquired skill will avail little, for he will find himself casting at a terrific rate, tying leader and line in knots, and doing everything but nice casting. Instead of laughing at him, however, the other contestants will praise him for one thing and offer a suggestion concerning another. Following these, he will be surprised to find his confidence returning, and the next time he tries to cast he will feel less timid and forget that he is being watched. Interest in the pastime will increase, and presently he will find that his interest in fishing is growing, and that it, too, presents allurements that he never thought of before.

There is not much that can be done during the winter in the way of fly-casting, but with bait-casting the case is different. In places where there is no water for summer practice, there will be found suitable ground for practice on the snow, and there many an otherwise dull afternoon may be pleasantly passed, with the bait or surf rod. The necessary equipment for this is simple. Determine on the place to stand in casting, which shauld be level with or slightly above the surface of the snow, as a low box or a couple of boards. Then with a tape measure off 100 feet, and drive a stake into the ground; to this attach the end of the tape, which, when stretched out another 100 feet, will furnish an accurate measure for all of your casts.

If two or more persons practice together, one may stand beyond the 100 foot mark while the others cast, and score for them, but if one casts alone, pieces of board or paper placed at 125, 150, 175, and 200 feet, will serve as marks by which he may determine his average distance casting—if he does not care, while reeling in, to walk up to the place where the weight falls each time, and mark the exact distance.

The lawn is also a fair place to practice, but casting on the snow is almost like practice on the water, and in it the line becomes more or less wet, so that it does not blister the thumb, as casting on the lawn with a dry line is likely to do until you have become accustomed to it.

It is well to keep an accurate score, be it good or bad, for this will show your improvement. Make one or two preliminary casts, then cast five times, scoring each cast, and divide the total by five, to obtain the average, marking the best single cast in each string, if you like. Count every cast made, marking those in which the reel overruns with a star, so that, later on, you can tell whether these backlashes come less frequently, as they should with practice. Do not try to excuse them, for backlashing is discouraging in bass casting, and in a tournament it ruins averages. Besides, if you could make five perfect casts at every trial, you would lose interest in the pastime. As in fishing, its uncertainty is one of its greatest charms.

There are plenty of mild days in winter when two or three friends may practice comfortably on the snow, and at this time uneven places that cannot be utilized when the ground is bare are admirable for casting. This is also a good time to locate a place for next season's club or group practice, and to make the necessary equipment. If a stream or a pond is convenient, locate a place for a platform, and even get the material for this in shape to be put into the water when spring comes.

If for a club of twenty members, and spectators are likely to number as many more when contests are held, there should be two platforms, arranged somewhat as follows (see Fig. 19).

SHORE L/NE BENCHES Off SEATS fOK f/S/ 70/TS.

Fig. 19.—Casting Platforms and Runways.

A represents a gangway at least twenty-five feet in length. B is a platform large enough to permit all of the club members to move about freely while arranging rods and lines; and, of course, interested visitors. It should be strongly supported, to prevent a collapse under the weight of a number of persons. C is a gangway at least fifteen feet in length, and D is the casting platform. This is placed at a distance from the main platform in order that a contestant while casting shall be free from all interference; a cross wind will not carry his line among his friends on the large platform, nor endanger the rods in the rack E. The platform will be close enough to the shore line for visitors to watch the casting, but they cannot bother the contestants nor endanger the rods and outfits.

It is obvious that the location of the platforms should be made with a view to taking advantage of the prevailing wind, the shore line being parallel with its course, so that casting may be with the wind. With platforms arranged as shown in Fig. 19, the marking line may be stretched to right or left, obliquely toward shore at either side, obliquely away from shore, and in bait-casting, straight away from shore. This latter direction would be unfavorable for fly-casting, as there would hardly be clear space for the back cast.

The referee should be stationed on the gangway C, and he should not permit any person to be with him while a contestant is on the small platform. This cannot well be less than 7x9 feet in size, and the regulation height is eighteen inches above the water level. Cover this platform with canvas, painted, to keep the lines clean and free from catching on splinters and nails.

The rod rack E should be four feet high, five feet long, and three feet wide, with notches on the top bar, to prevent rods from being blown over by the wind. Fig. 20 shows a convenient form for a rack.

Fig. 20.—Rod Rack.

H is the notched top bar, against which the rods lean, while the bar M prevents them from slipping. L is another cross-piece for rod forms and cases. Nails may be driven in the back bar of H, on which to hang coats and hats. If the rack is nailed down on the shore side of the platform, rods may rest against it securely, with leaders in the water, ready for casting.

Obviously the most reliable device with which to measure fly and bait casts is a string of floating boards with feet and inches marked on them; but these are costly and unwieldy. Next comes a line with floats attached, with the distances marked on them, or painted different colors, to represent various distances. The first device that suggests itself is an upright disk with figures painted on it, but this is impracticable because lines would catch on it, and the upright would need a counter-weight to prevent it from toppling over.

There must be no angles, projections or hooks for the lines to foul. The simplest line, therefore, is one consisting of 225 or 250 feet of 3-16 inch braided cord, such as tackle dealers sell for $1. 20 per 100 yards. A good grade of curtain cord is nearly as serviceable. Either one selected should be waterproof to prevent shrinking, stretching, and decay. To one end attach a harness snaphook, to be snapped into a ring on the forward edge of the casting platform. This hook must be put on last, as will appear farther on. Now measure off sixty feet and tie a simple knot in the line. Here let us digress for a moment.

Experience will prove that one who stands on the platform, occupied with his casting, cannot accurately determine how far he is casting a fly if the marking line is equipped with floats painted different colors. Neither can he see figures on the floats, all of which look alike to him, so fully occupied is he with his efforts to lengthen his casts. Make one mark round, another square, and so on, and he will at once associate the different forms with their proper distances. Egg-shaped floats are the most practical form, but the caster is at a disadvantage when they are employed, and if figures are painted on them, these cannot be seen easily by the judges when they are at a distance. Therefore, if the marks are five feet apart, which is close enough for a beginning, and for practice, let the first one at 60 feet be a six-inch red disk, with the figures painted in black on each side (R, Fig.2i)._

Bore the disk as shown, with a quarter-inch bit, so that the knot in the line will rest in the center. Dip two pine plugs in paint and drive them into the hole, one on each side, the ends flush with the disk. The knot in the line being between their ends, the disk cannot slip on the line, and the fresh paint will hold the plugs solidly. No matter which side of the disk is up, the figures may easily be seen by the judges, even at a distance.

Tie another knot five feet from the center of the first disk and attach a three-inch egg-shaped blue float, also plugged (S, Fig. 21). Five feet farther on attach a white disk, marked 70. At 75 feet use a square white disk bored from corner to corner; at 80 a white disk; at 85 a blue egg-shaped float; at 90 a white disk; at 95 another blue float; and at 100 another square white float (T, Fig. 21).

Fig. 21.—Floats for Marking Line.

This is about as far as the fly-caster can determine the form of floats accurately, unless they are somewhat widely separated. All that is now necessary is to provide for accurate scoring by the judges. White six-inch disks, therefore, will serve for the no, 120,130, 140, 160, 170, 180, and 190 foot marks, with large figures on each. At 125, 150, 175 and 200 feet use square floats, for the bait-casters can see these clearly. Paint the 125 and 175 foot marks red, the 150 and 200 foot marks white. Blue floats

mark the odd distances throughout the line, except at 75, 125, and 175 feet, as noted above. No weights of any sort will be needed, and if the corners and edges of all marks be smoothed off, there will be no place on the entire line that a casting line will foul.

These markers should all be saturated with linseed oil and dried before they are painted and marked, to prevent them from warping and checking. They should then be given two coats of enamel, not paint, and if taken out of the water after use, and stored in a dry place, they will remain clean and bright, and the figures will show distinctly. Such a line will cost about $5, and will last several seasons. White pine is best for the large marks. It should be one inch thick, and the square marks should be 12x12 inches. The egg-shaped floats can be purchased from tackle dealers.

For tournament use, where more accurate measurements are required, egg-shaped fishing floats i/ inches long can be used to mark every foot between the five and ten-foot distances.

Galvanized cable-laid steel wire one-eighth inch in diameter is better than braided cord. Attach all marks to this wire with painted pine plugs. Nails driven through markers and line are unsatisfactory.

For accuracy bait-casting a target is best. The simplest form may be made as follows: Join two ix4-inch boards in the center, as shown by KK, NN, Fig. 22, and paint them green. At their intersection attach a six-inch water-tight tin can (W), painted red. Encircling this, attach to the four bars a half-inch water-tight gas-pipe ring (P) 30 inches in diameter, painted white. Four staples may be used in making it fast to the bars. Wire will catch the lures. One foot from this circle attach a similar one 4 feet in diameter, and so on until five are in place. As all parts of the target should be just awash, with only the red bulls-eye showing distinctly, regulating devices are necessary. Four paint cans attached solidly to the bars underneath will serve, provided they do not leak. If the target floats too high, let a little water into the cans. Screw-top cans, are,

for this reason, the handiest form. (See X, Fig. 22.).
H
Fig. *22.* Fig. 23.
Accuracy Bait-Casting Target.

Some clubs have platforms so arranged that the accuracy target may be left afloat under the platform from week to week. Two sides of the platform are guarded with stakes, while on the ends there are hinged boards, made to turn down and lock, to prevent the target from being floated out and tampered with. It is a very handy arrangement, as a target of this size is awkward to carry to and from a storage place.

If the target must be carried any distance from where it is to be used, it may be made in sections (Fig. 23), and the segments put together by means of bolts through two of the bars (Z). In this case all ends of the tubes must be capped or plugged, to keep out water. The bullseye and air-tanks may be attached in various ways.

Under the target W (Fig. 22) attach a large screw-eye, and to this make fast the center of a suitable line. Attach snap-hooks to one part of the line, say 60, 80, and 100 feet from center of target. If the 6o-foot hook is made fast to the ring on the platform, the other end of the line is run through a pulley-block on a float anchored about no feet from the platform, then back to the platform, where it is belayed. When all contestants have finished casting at 60 feet, the 6o-foot snap is cast off, the yo-foot snap attached to the ring on the platform, then, by hauling on the other end of the line, the target is moved out to 70 feet, and so on up to 100 feet, the longest distance employed in accuracy casting. The line is in effect endless.

In casting at this target, if the lure falls on or within the 3O-inch circle, the cast is scored O, or perfect; if it falls within or on the next circle i demerit, and so on. Casts outside the largest circle are of course estimated. For example, if one scores a total of 50 demerits in fifteen casts—three at each distance, 60, 70, 80, 90, and 100 feet— divide it by 15, which gives 3 5/15. This, deducted from 100, gives a percentage of 96

10-15.

To waterproof braided or twisted lines used on targets, mix equal parts by weights of rosin, paraffin, beeswax, and linseed oil, stir well over a slow fire, and while very hot immerse the line in the solution for ten minutes. Wet a cloth, wring it out, and holding it in one hand over the mixture, draw the line through the cloth, stripping off all the surplus wax. Let the line cool and dry for a day or two before using.

CHAPTER XI FLY-CASTING CONTESTS
THERE is an old saying among the anglers-that it is easier to tell another person how to cast properly than to do the thing yourself. This, then, is my excuse for attempting to write of tournament casting; for I have practiced this amusement for less than fifteen years, and am just beginning to learn. But so many persons have asked me to tell them how I manage to cast 100 feet and more with a five-ounce rod that it is possible some notes on this subject may interest other anglers, too.

One of these inquirers told me—just what many old anglers have admitted— that he has fished for years, yet cannot cast more than sixty feet. Generally anglers think their rods and lines are not of the right sort, but it is human nature to overlook the real reason for lack of success in accomplishing the thing desired.

Practice casting with the fly-rod—or tournament casting, as it is generally called, to distinguish it from fishing—is good fun in season and out, but in addition to this, it is a great educator. One may be a successful fisherman for years without learning how to cast properly. He may adopt a style that is all wrong when it is just as easy to start right, as those do who are coached by expert casters until they acquire the knack of casting correctly. And after they have practiced a bit, they step into the trout stream with confidence in their rods and in themselves.

Tournament casting contests have been criticized severely by men who have not gone in for this sort of amusement on the ground that it is not fishing, and that the rods, reels, and lines used are not such as are commonly used in

fishing. This is mainly true; but still it is noticeable that every veteran fisherman who takes up casting becomes an enthusiast. A number of these veterans have told me that they learned more in one season on the platform than they had acquired in all the years they had been fishermen. And while I do not deny that many of the tools used in casting are made for that purpose, and are never taken to the stream, I do claim that every tournament rod, reel, and line can be used successfully in fishing in one place or another in this great country of ours. The tournament salmon rod is an excellent fishing rod; the heavy single-hand rod is used for grilse fishing—and more and more men are every year admitting that it is not necessary to swing a great English two-handed rod over salmon when they may be and are taken with ordinary medium to light weight trout rods; the five-ounce tournament rod is a favorite trout rod for large streams everywhere; and finally, the four-ounce tournament rod is one of the best dry-fly trout fishing rods that has been produced anywhere.

Aside from the practice in the company of good fellows who can and do make special efforts to assist one, to a fisherman the mingling with congenial spirits is an important part of club practice and contests. You may live in a village all your life and not know half the anglers there, but let some one start a casting club, and you will make the acquaintance of all the good fishermen roundabout, and form many lasting friendships at its meetings.

Take, for example, a tournament held in the autumn—one in which representatives of several casting clubs are contestants. On such occasions men are present who have just returned from fishing, and the discussions that arise their opinions are worth listening to. In the little visits that one has with them between contests, he is sure to learn something new and worth while in reference to fishing; for the angler, it must be conceded, never grows too old to learn.

At every casting tournament that I have attended—and I am sure that they were representative ones—half of those present were not contestants, but anglers who were drawn to those affairs because of the excellent opportunity offered to " talk fishing " with their fellows. In other words, to pick up information; to exchange ideas; to arrange future excursions to waters near or far. I know dozens of these men, who never cast, yet who are regular attendants, and mighty good judges of casting and of rods and tackle as well. And they claim that they learn something at every visit.

This defense of casting as a sport or game is made because it is sometimes ridiculed by those who have never considered the matter in the proper light, yet who would probably admit that, in order to become an expert game shot, it is necessary for one to practice at the target. You can hunt game with the rifle, and fish for trout with the fly-rod, without practice, but in both instances horse sense will show that it is better to attain proficiency through practice than to chuck and chance it without.

I will now attempt to give the beginner at flyfishing a few hints as to casting with ordinary fishing tackle, leaving tournament casting for discussion farther on.

CHAPTER XII FLY-FISHING PRACTICE THE best place to practice is on a pond or pool where a little point juts out from the shore, affording a clear space before and behind you, so that your line will not foul trees or bushes. Lacking this, erect a little platform from which to cast. Secure some planks or boards, then drive two stakes as far out as your boards will reach, nailing a strong cross-piece to them and making the ends of the boards fast to this. A second support nearer shore will be needed, to prevent the planks from springing too much. The width of the platform depends upon your own energy; two planks will serve, though six will be better.

The height may be only sufficient to clear the water. The regulation height for tournament platforms is eighteen inches above the water. This is all right for bait-casting, but for fly-casting it is an open question whether height is an advantage. I for one do not believe that it is. In distance casting the rod and line are kept at a considerable distance above the line of the caster's middle during the longest part of a cast. Control of the line is greatest when it is above the waist. Therefore, in my humble opinion, the nearer one stands to the water level, the better will be his control of the line.

If possible, cast along the shore, so that the floating marks may be placed at known distances, to inform you as to the progress you make; or so that some friend may tell you how far or how accurate are your casts.

Joint up your rod, attach the reel and thread the line through the guides and top. Attach a leader of ordinary length to the line, and put on an old fly with the hook cut off at the bend. A fairly heavy leader is best, and this should be well soaked and straightened.

It is conceded that a tapered line is employed, as this is the proper sort for fishing. The best size is E, but if the rod be powerful, with plenty of backbone, a D line may fit it better. By " fit " is meant that the weight of the heavier line will cause the rod to spring forward and back nicely when under perfect control of the wrist, and not compel you to put into the cast the full-arm motion that is so often seen, yet which is both unnecessary and fatiguing. Let the rod do the work.

Now, with the rod in the right and the line in the left hand, extend the line thirty feet; then draw it toward you gently until it straightens, and lift it quickly and cleanly, employing the wrist only, the arm resting against your side. The lift, retrieve, or recovery then steadies until the rod reaches the vertical position. Stop it there, for its work in retrieving ends at that point, and every degree it extends behind will detract materially from clean casting. Wait much longer than you ever did before on the back cast, then bring the rod forward with an even swing, and stop it dead just before it reaches the horizontal, at the same time letting a couple of yards of line run through the guides.

Try again, timing the cast and retrieve 1, 2; and the back cast 3, 4, 5, 6. Let a little more line out, and make a third essay, then strip in and rest. In stripping, or pulling, the line through the guides, always hold the tip of the rod down. Stripping with the rod held well up will soon ruin any line, as the latter is bent too much in passing through the top ring. This causes excessive wear and is unnecessary.

As you let more line out, you will notice that the rod works better—not stiffly, but like a flexible steel spring, the line seeming to be a part of it. This is as it should be. You will also notice that when you retrieve smartly, stop the rod overhead, wait patiently until the line pulls hard behind you, then make the forward cast without any snap at all— you will notice, I say, that considerably more line runs through your left hand, and that it lies out straight on the water without splash.

Remember that in fishing for trout that are shy, the less you disturb the water the better. Hence the value of learning to shoot the line instead of extending it by a series of casts, any one of which may frighten away your fish. " Shooting" means the jump the line makes at the end of the forward cast when the back cast is high up and properly timed.

Do not try to work out too far. It is better to work out in two or three casts, followed by a shoot, then strip in and begin over again. If you try repeatedly to lift all the line you can get out, you will only tire your wrist and make slovenly work of it.

Try again, but give attention to the left hand now. In the forward cast extend the left hand the right foot forward. At the end of the cast, and just before you begin to lift, pull in the line smartly until the left hand rests against the body. This will straighten the line on the water, and put it in motion to lift. This is a very important thing, for the full power of lifting is attained in this way, instead of wasting one-third of the retrieve in straightening a slack line.

No body motion is needed in cast or retrieve, though the involuntary slight bending forward and backward is not objectionable. The right arm from the elbow up might as well be tied against the side, for its function is merely to steady the wrist. The thumb performs an important function, too. Do not grasp the rod as you would an umbrella handle —as some anglers do—but keep the thumb parallel with the grasp. In this position the thumb helps materially in stopping the rod at the end of the back cast, and in keeping the rod at the proper angle. Do not cant the rod toward the right, but retrieve and cast straight over the right shoulder. This makes for accuracy.

Of course the side cast should be practiced, too, for there are places where the overhead cast cannot be employed, as in wading along a shore overhung with low growth. Later on it will be well to practice casting with the left hand. There are many times when one must use the right hand to help himself over or around difficult places, and when that hand tires it is a comfort to shift the work to the left hand. But the overhead cast is the proper one to master first, then the others will be learned quickly.

In making a fishing cast hold the left hand rigid; or, as some do, hook the second finger of the right hand over the line, so that it may be kept taut and under perfect control, else the fly will be snapped back or the line will lay out slack with a splash. The same thing may occur in a shoot if too much line is let out, or if it is checked abruptly.

It is difficult to learn to shoot the line until you have succeded in casting forty or fifty feet. The reason for this is that you do not get out enough of the belly of the line to act as a weight, which, on being projected by the spring of the rod, shoots forward in a rolling loop, as shown in Fig. 24, pulling several feet of Fig. 24.—Rolling Loop of Line at End of Forward Cast line with it. In order to fix in your mind just how this is done, ask a companion to take hold of the fly, and walking alongshore, say fifty feet, release it at the word, when you begin to retrieve. If the back cast is given plenty of time, the line will go forward with enough force to pull ten

or more feet of line through the guides, and shoot the fly considerably farther than you had before been able to cast it. From this you will also understand that it is the resistance of the water on the line in retrieving that brings out the full spring of the rod. As a result the line is thrown high up behind you in a loop just the reverse of that shown in Fig. 24. The common error is to carry the rod too far back (Fig. 25), the line

Fig. 25.—Back Cast in Which the Line Strikes the Water Behind.

touching or lying out on the water behind you, making " sloppy work " of the next forward, cast.

Carrying the rod too far back is generally followed by starting the forward cast too soon. The line is not given time to straighten behind. When the forward cast is started with the fly in position indicated in Fig. 25, the line straightens with a whip-like snap, and often the fly is cut off. But when the rod is stopped correctly, the line is thrown back high up, and Fig. 26 illustrates its position when plenty of

Fig. 26.—Position of Line and Fly at end of Back Cast, time has been given to let the line and leader turn over and begin to fall—the proper moment to start the forward cast. The line will then roll out cleanly and alight softly. Fig. 27 shows how the line looks at the middle of the forward cast, the fly passing over your head.

Fig. 27.—Forward Cast. Granted that it is not often that you will have occasion to make fishing casts of more than forty or fifty feet, it is nevertheless well to be able to cast farther than that. For every ten feet that you increase your average distance, the difficulty of manipulating rod, line, and fly cleanly will increase. To master these obstacles and gain confidence in yourself and your tackle is worth a great deal more to you, even though you may never need to cast more than forty feet in your fishing. Perfect mastery of a long line counts when you fish under trees, for if you can control a long line in the open, it will be easier to manipulate a short line without getting " hung up." Therefore, practice diligently. And as it is a great advantage

to know if you are progressing, rig up a line by means of which you can measure your casts roughly, and at the same time aim for precision. Three wooden disks each six inches in diameter will serve. Coat them with enamel, so they will show more plainly in the water than if painted. Make them red, white, and blue, respectively. Take an old fishing line and measuring off fifty feet, tie on a bit of red string. Ten feet farther attach a piece of white string, for sixty feet; and blue string at the seventy-foot mark. Wind the line on an old reel, making the platform end fast to the axle. In use, reel off the line, tie the disks on at the proper places, and stretch the line from platform to shore, or anchor the outer end with a stone. Besides helping you in distance work, the disks will be excellent marks for accuracy casting.

With any good fly-rod you can cast seventy feet or more if you will keep in mind constantly the principal points: straighten the line with the left hand, lift quickly, stop the rod overhead, give the back cast plenty of time, and carry the forward cast through steadily without the common but objectionable snap at the end. Practice will do the rest, but if you cast in company with other anglers, ask one of them to assist you in timing the back cast. If he will tell you when you carry the rod too far back, and you will wait with the back cast until he says, " Now," you will soon succeed in correcting your faults and in increasing your distance. At the same time you will have acquired confidence in yourself and your tackle.

Besides the overhead cast and the side cast, which is only a modification of the former, it will be worth while to learn the switch cast. In fishing it is often impossible to employ the back cast, because of a high bank or trees behind you. The switch cast overcomes these difficulties. Learn it by all means.

Make a cast, and instead of lifting the line, carry the rod up slowly to the vertical, then go forward and downward with speed and force. The line will be pulled toward you on the water until the fly is say fifteen feet distant, then projected forward with a snap that will carry the fly clear of the water, to alight cleanly farther and farther at every cast. The style is just the reverse of ordinary casting. Retrieve slowly, cast quickly, and repeat until the desired distance is attained. At no time need rod, line, or fly pass more than three feet behind you.

Dry-fly casting is so fascinating and so useful that every angler should practice it. It differs in style from wet-fly casting in that the water is not touched by fly or line until sufficient distance has been attained to place the fly at a certain point. Start with a short line and cast up and out, back and forward, letting a little line out with each false cast, until sufficient line is out, then cast lightly on the water and let the fly float. Retrieve very gently, and make several false casts, to dry the fly and extend the line, before making another fishing cast. The back and forward casts are both made in about equal time, and care is taken to prevent the fly from touching the water on the retrieve. It will assist you if you will use your disks as targets. Start with the line the length of the rod, making several false casts, then a scoring cast at the first mark; three or four dry casts, then score at the second mark, and so on. This is pretty work, and good fishing practice.

Five targets are used in dry-fly accuracy contests, each one a thirty-inch circle. Wooden barrel hoops attached to a line will serve. The standard distances for light rods are 20, 271/2, 35, 424 and 50 feet. Three scoring casts are made at each target, with at least one false cast in between. A cast inside the circle counts o, or perfect; within one foot of the circle, I demerit; within two feet, 2 demerits, and so on; If the fly fails to float, I additional demerit. If you score 60 demerits, divide 60 by 15, the number of casts, giving 4; deducting 4 from loo gives the percentage, 96.

A few words regarding rods may not be out of place here. For all-round trout fishing a rod of five or six ounces is perhaps best, and the favorite length is 9 or 9*y* feet; but quicker rods are now used than formerly, though it is possible to carry stiffness to extremes. There are

few prettier rods to fish the fly with than those having slow action, and although the stif-fer rods are better for windward work and for fishing the floating fly, if you can have only one rod, see that it has good action clear down to the hand.

The five-ounce tournament rod is a splendid one for heavy streams not much overgrown, but as these rods are generally ten feet long, they are not so handy for brooks as the three-and four-ounce rods of 8 or 9 feet. For dry-fly work the four-ounce, 9-foot tournament rod is ideal. It works best with a tapered D line.

CHAPTER XIII TOURNAMENT LINES THE fishing practice casting of which I have written leads naturally to tournament casting; or, in other words, to competition, between two friends, it may be, or among members of a fishing club. When two persons practice together a third frequently puts in appearance, and ere long the fascination of the pastime is discussed, with the result that a club springs into being. No costly equipment or grounds being necessary, it is not difficult to find a pond or pool suitable for practice, and plenty of willing hands to put together platform, marking line, and targets.

Fishing rods are used at first, and then one by one the members procure tournament rods and lines. As in all other games, the rules being liberal enough to admit anything within reason, it follows that no one wishes to be outclassed if good tackle will prevent it.

In distance trout fly-casting, rods of several types are recognized. The so-called heavy rod is limited only as to length—n feet; but it must of course be held in one hand only. This is the most popular rod. Its weight ranges from 9 to 13 ounces, the average being about 10 ounces.

The five-ounce rod comes next. If it has a metal reel-seat it may weigh just under 54 ounces. There is no restriction as to length, but 10 feet is the popular maximum length. This is the " most rod " of any, for its ounces. The fittings are made light, so that all possible weight may be put into the cane. It is used more and more every year, both for fishing

and contest casting. It is used for wet-fly distance; for dry-fly distance; for dry-fly accuracy; and for wet-fly accuracy.

The 424-ounce rod—a distinctively Eastern rod—is coming into more general use. Perhaps it will be the all-round rod of the future. Nine feet is the popular length, and so powerful is this little rod that it is frequently called upon to handle the very heavy lines suited to 10-ounce rods—lines that weigh almost half as much as the rod. So far this rod has been used only in wet-fly distance casting, and in dry-and wet-fly trout fishing.

Several years ago the National Association was asked to, and did pass, a rule limiting the salmon rod length to 15 feet. The object was to fix on a reasonable length, and to encourage salmon anglers to use the,ir fishing rods in contests. Until then one could go into a salmon event with a bean pole, if he cared to, or use one of the ridiculous 18- or 20-foot English rods, weighing several pounds. That the 15-foot rule is a good one has been proved on several occasions, when casters have, with rods of this length, exceeded the best records ever made by Britishers with rods of any length. In fact, our cousins across the water have never made much of a showing in distance fly-casting. Perhaps this accounts for the efforts some of them make to poke fun at our tournament fly-rods.

That salmon casting is not a giant's game is shown by the excellent records made by men far under the average in height and weight. But salmon rods are costly, and few individuals care to purchase rods solely for use in two or three contests yearly. Where clubs furnish these rods, however, as some do, the contests are always well patronized. These rods weigh from 24 to 28 ounces.

The five-ounce rod being an excellent one to start with, let us see what you can do with it.

The first thing to be provided is a line. You can cast during your novitiate with a regular double tapered line, but there is something better. The fishing line is thirty yards long. As the taper on each end is from twelve to eighteen feet, the total length must be made up by a level middle, or belly. With a line of this sort you can work out just so far, and there you are stopped because the belly of the line is too heavy to shoot.

The logical thing to do is to cut the line, splice a length of small level line on to the belly, for a back (or shooting) line, and make the front taper longer, by splicing a few feet of level line on the end.

So far, so good; but what must be the proportions of leader, taper, belly, back line? you ask. If I knew just how far you could cast three times out of four, I could give you exact formulae; but as I do not, the only thing left is to strike an average. In handicapping contestants it is customary in some clubs to place one who has no record in the seventy-five foot class; that is, on the safe assumption that he will cast that far, at least, with a little practice. Make up a line based on that rule.

With this line you can work out until the rear end of the belly is in your hand or on the rod, but not farther up than the middle joint. When that point is reached you must either shoot or strip in, for you cannot lift the line if the belly runs off the rod. You measure, then, from where you stand to the sixty-five-foot mark, thus allowing ten feet on the safe side of seventy-five feet.

We will say that the leader is to be six feet long, for a starter. Twenty-five feet is a good length for the front taper. The proportions are, then:

Leader 6 feet

Front taper *25* feet

Belly 34 feet 65 feet

This is the key to an endless number of combinations that you may work out as you become more proficient—measure from where you stand to the point where you can cast regularly. If you increase the length of the taper, decrease the length of the belly, and vice versa; it being understood, of course, that you will add to the length of one or both as your skill is augmented. But as thirty-five yards is a good length, add forty feet of fine level line to your casting line.

If you know how long each taper of your fishing line is, you will be able to splice a piece on one end long enough to make that taper twenty-five feet. If not, try a piece ten feet long, then measure back sixty-five feet, cut the line there and splice on the back line, which should be a good piece of level dressed line, But as you will soon " out-grow" this first line, do not cut up a good fishing line, but purchase a regulation tournament line or make up one from several lengths of the proper sizes.

The tournament lines are made in various ways, but two of the most frequently used are like this: One tapers up almost the full length to the center, then tapers down to the other end; the other has a long front taper, a belly ranging from twenty to fifty feet, then tapers down rapidly to a thin, level back line. This type of line has proved to be the best one for distance casting.

If you are fond of experimenting, make up a line from pieces of level dressed line, which you can purchase in twenty-five-yard lengths, splicing the various pieces together. In this it is of course desirable to make few splices, hence the tapers will not be nicely graduated, but this will not greatly matter in practice. If the thirty-four-foot belly is size B, splice fifteen feet of D on the front end, and a ten-foot length of F on D. Then on the back end of the belly splice on five feet of D and the forty-foot back line. Four splices only will be needed, as against twice as many if the tapers be graduated nicely.

In making splices, fray out the ends to be joined, using a needle or any pointed instrument. Pick the strands apart carefully for three-quarters of an inch, then separate them into two equal parts as shown in Fig. 28. Join

Fig. 28.—Frayed Ends of line Ready for Splicing. the pieces, but do not push them together tight, as a hard, thick splice will be the result. The four ends will overlap sufficiently to make a splice that will not pull apart.

Wax a length of silk thread, and commencing at the center of the splice, secure one end of the thread against slipping (Fig. 29) while you When the frayed ends of the line are covered, lay a loop of thread along the line, wind over loop a half-dozen turns, then pull end of silk under and wind the opposite end in the same fashion. Roll the finished splice under a ruler, to make it smooth, and apply two coats of shellac. A splice of this sort will last a long time if shellacked when it shows signs of wear. It is smooth, and with practice you will be able to make it almost as small as the line itself.

Fig. 29.—Winding the Splice. wind one-half of the splice with the other.

In casting a spliced line will last a long time if you do not strip in line while the rod is held upright. Always keep the rod down in stripping. Otherwise the waterproof dressing will be damaged at the rod top every time the line is pulled sharply enough to bend it at an angle.

If you find that the taper of your spliced line is not what it should be, in your opinion, you can take the line apart and change it until it suits you; or if the front end becomes worn, discard a section and put in a new one, make the taper longer or shorter, etc. Splices are not difficult to make, but if you have a fly-tyer's vise it is advisable to use it in holding the line. Better winding will result.

For splicing, and for all rod and tackle repairs, a bit of wax is a necessity. It is easily made, as follows: Melt together over a slow fire in a small tin dish or cup, one ounce of rosin and twenty grains of beeswax. Stir with a stick, then add sixty grains of fresh, unsalted lard, or lacking this, an equal quantity of mutton tallow. Stir for several minutes, then pour the mixture into a basin of cold water. Rub a little vaseline on your fingers, to prevent the wax from sticking to them at first, take it out of the water and pull and work it until it becomes cream color, then put it in a piece of chamois skin, and it is ready for use.

Theodore Gordon, who has had a very wide experience in fishing and fly-tying, has given me the following recipe for silk wax. I have found it excellent. The variations are for different seasons:

No. i. Rosin 2 ounces, lard Bounce,

paraffin wax i drachm.

No. 2. Rosin 2 ounces, paraffin wax %-ounce, lard I drachm.

No. 3. Rosin 2 ounces, paraffin wax %-ounce, lard 2 scruples.

No. 4. Rosin 2 ounces, paraffin wax %-ounce, lard *y* -drachm.

Work while under cold water and wrap in chamois skin.

Do not wind your spliced line—or any other —on a fishing reel, but use something larger. In tournament casting a great many anglers use a " reel" (Fig. 30) turned from a piece of

Fig. 30.—Reel for Tournament Fly Lines. Any wood worker can turn this from a piece of poplar or white pine. Its diameter is 9 inches; thickness, I inch; width of rim, 14 inches; depth of groove, J4 inch; width of groove, 24 inch. It will hold any fly line. Protect it from warping and checking with two coats of shellac. A loop of cord is attached to end of line, then looped over the loop, pulled taut, then the casting line rolled on.

I-or i4-inch white pine or poplar. This is simply a disk seven or eight inches in diameter with a groove cut in its edge and the center cut out, leaving a sort of grooved hoop. It will hold a large quantity of the heaviest line. With it the line is reeled in very rapidly. Its principal advantage is that its diameter being large, the line is not cramped, but comes off straight and runs through the guides like a lead wire.

The chief fault with these wooden reels is that they split readily if dropped. In casting about for something as light but stronger I hit on the following plan.

Two pieces of sheet aluminum, 7x7x11/16-inches were purchased. On each one I scribed two circles, one 7 inches, the other *$y* inches in diameter. They were easily cut out with a hacksaw, the inner edges smoothed with file and emery cloth, the outer edges with a very small plane. Two feet of thin brass tubing, and three feet of soft brass wire just the size to fit the tubing were then procured. The tubing was sawed into 4-inch lengths, and the wire into %-inch lengths. I then marked the inner edge of one of the aluminum circlets in six-

teen places, evenly spaced, and clamping them together in a vise, bored holes through both at the marks, and just far enough away from the edge so that the rivets would not pull out.

Taking the circlets out of the vise, they were placed, one on each end of a piece of tubing, a piece of wire pushed through all, and both ends riveted. This was done all-round, the ends of rivets smoothed off, and I had a reel that is practically indestructible, but which weighs about four ounces. Being open on two edges, the line dries nicely on the reel, and it will hold a great deal of line. By the use of the pieces of tubing and wire I was saved the labor of making rivets from solid wire, but the reel is strong and neat, and I have several of them that have seen hard use for a number of years. They are made to fit one within the other.

After using these reels for some time, William Mills & Son asked permission to copy them, and they put out reels that are of course far superior to mine, as theirs are made from spun aluminum, practically in one piece. They are made up in sets of two or three, one fitting within the other.

In stringing up the rod, in casting, the reel is placed on the platform. The line is unrolled from the reel as one would do with a tape measure but never pulled off in coils, as this would snarl it.

The calibers of fishing lines, as made by the different firms, are almost hopelessly confused. Some firms use what seems to be the original method—of employing the first nine letters of the alphabet—and others use nine figures. Then some reverse the order, so that a No. 6 line, say, is larger than a No. i. Then again lines are numbered arbitrarily, so that a No. 3 and a *Photograph by George A. Irwitt*

Bait-Casting for Bass in Florida

No. 269 are alike in caliber but different in style of braiding or finish.

An interesting paragraph on the subject of line calibers was given by Theophilus South in his " Fly-Fishers' Textbook," (London, 1841), as follows:

"Salmon Reel Lines.—Now, as to these, they should be from sixty to

eighty yards long— you require the latter length especially where salmon incline to run much, and from your contiguity to trees or bushes on the bank, you cannot follow him or change your position. Another advantage is that as the end which is so much on the water and so constantly passing through the rings of the rod in shortening and lengthening your throw can never be depended on for soundness above one season at most, removing the damaged part, sufficient length still remains for ordinary rivers and places, while a joint or splice in the line should always be avoided, if feasible.

" The material, I repeat, should be silk and hair twisted, and the end, for about twelve yards, may taper slightly; though perhaps it is as well to have it of uniform substance throughout, of about the thickness of the 'D ' in the third octave of your sister's harp (to measure which, borrow her string gauge), or thinner than a new shilling, which is strong enough for any salmon anywhere, provided it is used skilfully. Many old and experienced salmon fishers adopt much stouter, yet I prefer fine fishing, and am ready, for a wager to kill any fish under fifty pounds in a tolerable situation with the substance I allude to. It will bear at least eighteen pounds dead weight, and perhaps more.

" Trout reel lines should be of the same material; namely, twisted hair and silk, but necessarily much thinner, and from thirty to fifty yards in length, or even longer for lake fishing, where heavy trout are expected. However, thirty yards is quite enough for a light trout rod. They must taper gradually for the last eight or ten yards to the end, where, in substance, they should not exceed the first ' D' on the aforesaid harp guage, or very thick netting silk, while the stouter end should be about equal to the second ' D '."

For a number of years I have been collecting data on the subject of line calibers, and in my own work I follow these sizes:

Number Inch Number Inch
No. 2 or o/o 065 E 038
A 060 F 034

B 056 G 030
C 052 H 026
D 045 I 021

These sizes have been compared with those employed by a very large number of British, Scotch, and American makers and dealers. The average variation is so slight that they have been found very satisfactory.

To assist those who do not possess micrometer calipers, but have access to the standard wire guage, the following table may be of interest. It is that adopted by Brown & Sharpe, and is known as the American wire guage.

Number Inch Number Inch 14 064 20 03I IS 057 21 028 l6 OSO 22 02S 17 045 23 022 18 040 24 020 19 035 CHAPTER XIV TOURNAMENT FLY-CAST-ING NOW we are ready to commence casting. String up the five-ounce rod, but place the reel behind you on the platform at your left, and after unreeling all the line, coil it back, so that it will render freely through your left hand and the guides. Stand with your right foot forward, and make it a habit to move your feet only when necessary, and then with due care for the line on the platform. It is an old joke with casters that a line will not shoot well when you are standing on it!

Make a couple of casts, working the line out thirty or forty feet. In the next cast lift the line smartly the instant that it touches the water, giving it no time to " drown." The left hand assists at the same time by straightening the line on the water, so that it is moving toward you as you begin to retrieve. These are very important first steps, and should be practiced diligently. Keep in mind the fact that by pulling the line in with the left hand you put the full strength of the rod into lifting a tight line. Remember, too, that you cannot lift a long line if you wait until it sinks, or drowns.

In picking up quickly and in stopping the rod when it reaches the vertical, you will be able to keep the line high up in the back cast, and this will give the line plenty of time to straighten and go forward without touching anything, The higher the back cast, the more time you can give it—and you will seldom wait

too long. When the line pulls hard, start the forward cast, carrying it through steadily but without snap, stopping the rod just above the horizontal. At the same time let a little line run through the guides. Then pull in, lift with a vim, and wait patiently for the pull behind. On the next cast, if you feel the small line in your hand, let the line run, and do not retrieve. We will call this a scoring cast.

In shortening line you can strip in several yards, then lift, but in a contest this wastes time, and when you have only five or eight minutes in which to do your best casting, every second is valuable. Therefore, strip in ten or fifteen feet, then make a strong switch cast, followed by a quick lift. If the cast that follows be a good one, and the line pulls nicely in the back cast, shoot for a scoring cast. Do not hurry, take plenty of time, but do not waste any of it trying to lift too much line. It is better policy to try to make one scoring cast per minute. The fault most common to casters is too great haste. While the switch cast helps materially in " getting under " a long line, it should be practiced often, for it tires the wrist very much more than does the overhead cast.

In tournament casting it is necessary to depart from your fishing style and put the entire arm into service. In the forward cast you bend forward slightly and carry the right arm as far out as possible. Then in retrieving straighten up, pull in all the line you can manage with the left hand, and carry the right hand high above you, but not far enough to let the rod go back more than five degrees beyond the vertical. It will of course spring back with the line, but ask a friend to coach you, to assist you in learning the difficult feat of stopping the rod as it must be stopped if you are to become a distance caster. It is very difficult to do this, for it puts severe strain on the thumb and wrist, but you will see the advantage if you will watch a caster who frequently strikes the tip of his rod on the platform behind him, as some do at first.

It is considered very bad form to touch the water on the back cast with

line or leader. In addition to this, to touch or strike on the back cast ruins the forward cast, and what is worse, it is possible to smash the tip or middle joint of the rod by lifting the line when it drops on the water behind you.

It will assist you in learning to stop if you will practice with a rod having a long grasp. Push the butt inside your sleeve and cast with rigid arm. Stop arm at the right place and note the difference; the rod will not go back, it being held by your sleeve. This is not permitted in contests, and it is well to use the rod just as it comes from the maker, but trying this method will do no harm in practice.

At first you will find the line and leader troublesome. You will tie both in innumerable knots and end perhaps, in a hopeless tangle. As the loop of the line and the leader pass each other frequently in a series of casts, it is not remarkable that one should foul the other. The remedy is consistent practice, carrying the rod forward and back straight over the right shoulder. Attempting to lift too much line may snarl it, for sooner or later you will lose control of it, and in the threshing that generally follows, a bad tangle will end the matter. Veterans frequently mention the time when, as they say, they were consistent in lifting ninety feet of line for every cast of eighty feet 1 Learn to shoot, as that is the secret of all distant casting. With a properly balanced tournament line it is seldom necessary to lift more than eighty feet of line in order to make a cast of one hundred feet, and it is possible at times to shoot the line much farther than twenty feet. Work out until the small back line is reached, then hold the line there, wait for a good back cast, and shoot. Strip in and try again.

One of the chief faults in distance casting is the putting of too much strength into the forward cast. Too many casters try to " slam " the line, and this slam ends with a snap that carries the rod into or near the water, effectually killing the shoot. They have no point of aim, as the archers say. Practice until you can keep this in mind at every cast. Fix your attention on some distant

Lightning Source UK Ltd.
Milton Keynes UK
UKOW04f1223030517
300391UK00010B/399/P

object that appears to be about thirty feet higher than the loo-foot mark. Aim for that point, and never let the rod tip go below it. If you end the cast with a snap, the tip of the rod vibrates violently at the very instant when it should stop dead in order to permit the line to slide freely through the guides in the shoot.

Look at the matter from another angle. It is the perfect back cast that makes for a long shoot, and when the back cast is right, you will be surprised to see how far you can shoot if you will merely carry the rod forward to the stopping point—"lay it down," as the saying goes. In eight minutes casting time in an event, it is a severe penalty to be compelled to devote five minutes to replacing lost flies—and you are sure to snap the fly off if you hurry with the back cast and slam the Tine. Again, let the rod do the work; that is what is was made for. It will lift the heavy line, stop it, and start it going again. Merely keep the line going until gravity stops the farther progress of the belly, and the force that has been properly applied will carry the taper and leader on and out, to turn over in a graceful loop, and lay out straight on the water.

Hold the line until the rod reaches the stopping point, then let it run. Too many casters let go of the line before the completion of the cast. The result is that line and leader fall into a heap, or the leader doubles back. The forward cast with fly-and bait-rod is very much alike. With the latter you carry the cast through steadily, raise the thumb and let the line run out. With the fly-rod you release the line when the belly begins to pull.

Long tapers are popular for distance casting, but it is not advisable to go to extremes in this matter. In a place where the air is dry, a much longer taper may be used successfully than in places where the air is heavy and humid. Twenty-five feet is a good length; thirty feet can be managed by the average caster; thirty-five feet will suit one who is in the ninety-foot class; and forty feet

is about all that any caster will be able to master in heavy air. Too often the taper is slow at the point and quick at the back end—next to the belly. It should be just the reverse, for if it is spun out too fine it will not straighten, particularly if there is a side wind, or eddying currents of air near the water.

Experiment with leaders until you are sure that you can always straighten one of a certain length. If this is twelve feet long, keep an eight-foot leader in reserve for an unfavorable day. The best tapered leaders you can afford are none too good for distance casting. If you cannot straighten a short leader, cut a foot off the line taper and try again. Failing, cut off six inches more. Go slow with this, and try it on different days before spoiling the taper.

It is a common fault to use a line that is too heavy for the rod. B is heavy enough for the five-ounce rod if the belly is thirty to thirty-five feet in length. A thirty-five-yard B tournament line should weigh ijHi ounces to $i/2$ ounces. For dry-fly distance casting with the five-ounce rod, and for wet-fly distance casting with the four-ounce rod, a C line weighing 4 ounces is about right. Less belly and taper are needed in the last-named line.

What has been said of casting with the five-ounce rod applies both to the four-ounce and the unlimited rod. The latter is generally $li/2$ feet long, and is fitted with a long grasp. Bare your arm and lay it down on a two-foot rule. Measure from the end of the thumb to a point on the muscles of the forearm $2/2$ inches from the point of the elbow. This will determine the proper length of the grasp, say from 13 to 15 inches. (See Fig. 31.)

Fig. 31.—Position of Arm and Hand in Casting With the Unlimited Rod.

In selecting a rod, see that it has good action clear down to the hand. If it is too stiff it will force you to cast rapidly, and this you cannot do with a heavy rod. The middle joint should be strong, and the tip of slow rather than quick taper.

Of the two, a rod with stiff butt, and one with apparently too much butt action, choose the latter. Give no heed to the weight of the rod, save that it should in a measure correspond with your strength. Mere weight signifies little in the unlimited rod, and one weighing 9 ounces may suit you better than one of ii or 12 ounces.

In selecting the rod with which I have done my best general average distance casting, I did so with the intention of trying a lighter one than any of the four rods that I had used during several seasons. The one I finally selected had very slow action, and seemed to weigh less than ten ounces. In practice it did not tire my arm, would lift a very long line, and one day I weighed it. The old rods weighed 12, 11%, 12, and n4 ounces respectively; the new one $12J/2$ ounces!

For greater convenience in stripping the line, the lowermost, or hand guide, should be thirty to thirty-six inches from the butt of the rod. It is well to have a hand guide of phosphor bronze, steel, or agate, as this guide is subjected to excessive wear. I prefer bronze for the reason that agates are so easily broken. And agate tops are an abomination. The other guides should be snake pattern and a little larger than those of the fishing rod. Bronzed steel guides are best.

In casting with the heavy rod, hold the butt against the muscles of the forearm, thumb extended along the grasp, wrist absolutely rigid. (Fig. 31.). Cast just as you would if the grasp were lashed to your hand and arm. The only hinges are at the elbow and shoulder.

You lift the line with the whole arm; you stop the rod with rigid arm and wrist, keeping the butt against the forearm. This is a difficult thing to master, but it can and must be done. I find it a help to use a soft rubber buttcap, which prevents the butt from slipping off the forearm in lifting the line. I use one of the caps made for bait rods, but trim it down until it is the same diameter as the handgrasp.